HAUNTED
SAN JOSE

HAUNTED
SAN JOSE

ELIZABETH KILE

Haunted
America

Published by Haunted America
A division of The History Press
Charleston, SC
www.historypress.com

Front cover: Author photo.
Back cover: 1900, San Jose, Alum Rock Park meteor. Courtesy of San Jose Public Library, California Room, Clyde Arbuckle Photograph Collection.

First published 2022

Manufactured in the United States

ISBN 9781467150811

Library of Congress Control Number: 2022937932

To Nicole, my partner in paranormal adventures,
and to Anna and Lila, my storytellers

CONTENTS

Preface   9
Acknowledgements   11
Introduction   13

1. LOCAL LANDMARKS   15
   Hayes Mansion   15
   Winchester Mystery House®   20
   Chuck E. Cheese   26
   Kelley Park / Happy Hollow   28

2. SCHOOLS   32
   Arbuckle Elementary   32
   Bernal Intermediate   34
   Del Mar High   37
   Dove Hill Elementary   39
   Independence High   40
   Muwekma Ohlone Middle   43
   Notre Dame High   44
   Overfelt High   47
   Piedmont Hills High   48
   Silver Creek High   49
   Slonaker Elementary   51

CONTENTS

3. SAN JOSE STATE UNIVERSITY   52
   Hoover Hall   52
   Joe West Hall   55
   Yoshihiro Uchida Hall   56

4. HOTELS   60
   Sainte Claire Hotel   60
   The Fairmont   62
   Le Baron Hotel / Holiday Inn Silicon Valley 65

5. RESTAURANTS AND NIGHTLIFE   68
   65 Post Street / Splash Video Dance Bar   68
   Trials Pub   71
   Grandview Restaurant   73
   Jose Theatre / San Jose Improv   75

6. PARKS   79
   Santa Teresa Springs / Dottie's Pond   79
   Almaden Winery Park   84
   Alum Rock Park   87

7. ROADS   93
   San Felipe Road   93
   Quimby Road   95
   Hicks Road   98

8. NEW ALMADEN   103
   La Forêt Restaurant   104
   Hacienda Cemetery   105

9. PRIVATE HOMES   109
   Park Avenue   109
   Hellyer House   112
   Doerr-Steindorf Neighborhood   115

Bibliography   117
About the Author   127

PREFACE

San Jose is a place where the past and the future converge. From its humble beginnings in 1777 as a riverside pueblo, to its significant agricultural production around the turn of the twentieth century, to its current leadership in technological innovation, San Jose has the weight of history behind it, along with the ability to look forward and imagine what might be next. This blend of credibility and creativity seems to nurture paranormal activity, allowing ghosts to inhabit spaces both historical and modern and make themselves known to the living.

The city is also, to some degree, responsible for my own lifelong interest in the paranormal. I am a seventh-generation Californian. My first San Jose family member was born here in 1798, only twenty-two years after the city's founding. Because of my family's deep connection to the city's roots, I grew up immersed in San Jose's history. And, in part, because of my mother's casual interest in the paranormal, I grew up captivated by ghost stories and legends. My fascination has led me to seek out haunted locations and to participate in paranormal investigations but also to uncover the history behind the stories, to learn more about the people and places that populate the tales and try to get to the genesis of the hauntings.

I am a believer in ghosts, but I also consider myself a skeptic, looking for rational explanations and relying on common sense. But there are things that can't be simply explained away, and a couple of experiences have convinced me that there is something beyond our realm of normal understanding—the very definition of paranormal. I like to think that this blend of skepticism and belief makes the unexplainable more compelling: if I don't see ghosts everywhere I look, then, when I do experience something I can't explain, I'm much more apt to believe in it.

To that end, this book doesn't shy away from debunking some persistent claims that run counter to the historical record. That doesn't mean that ghosts don't exist or that the locations aren't haunted. It does mean that sometimes the legends have taken on lives of their own and some distinction should be made between lore and fact. Part of the pleasure of sharing ghost stories is in the telling, not necessarily in the believing. If a story is compelling and frightening enough, does it matter if it's true? Probably not. We can continue to scare ourselves with stories we know are implausible, but out of respect for those who came before us, we should also acknowledge the historical record.

This book is meant to be a blend of history and mystery. In many cases, the historical background is just as fascinating as the stories of ghosts and hauntings, so I've taken pleasure in exploring that history. It's also important to honor our predecessors by keeping them alive in our memory. Just as we hope future generations will be interested in us and the way we live, those who lived before us shared the same desire not to live and die anonymously. It's human nature to want to be remembered. After all, isn't that why ghosts continue to make their presence known?

ACKNOWLEDGEMENTS

It's a cliché, but writing is a lonely endeavor. Writing a book about ghosts in a hyper-scientific society that doesn't want to talk about ghosts is an extreme exercise in loneliness and frustration. The difficulty I had in getting people to talk to me about haunted San Jose reminds me that this continues to be a taboo subject. So, to that end, I am extremely grateful to those who took a risk or were curious or open-minded enough to discuss their experiences with me, namely, Windy Abreau-Campen, Danny Diaz, Stefen Grace, Marilyn Jerkovich, Allen Weitzel and those who contacted me via email or social media to share stories that didn't end up in the book.

I am also grateful to those who may not have had ghost stories of their own but offered me tremendous support as I was writing:

Laurie Krill at The History Press, thank you for your support through the process.

Nicole Hughes, thank you for helping me with quite literally everything, even before I knew I was writing a book. This book couldn't have happened without your literary and marketing expertise, your unwavering cheerleading and your hilarious skepticism. You're the best writing and traveling buddy—paranormal or otherwise—I could hope for.

My children have been to more parts of San Jose and more haunted locations than most people their age. Thank you for keeping me company; it's so much fun to take you places. You can read this book when you're older.

Thanks to both of my parents for filling our home with books and always reminding me I am a writer.

A specific thanks to my mom, for helping me with history, social media and childcare and for introducing me to all things spooky and ghostly when I was probably too young for them.

Wesley, thanks for holding down the fort and for listening to more stories than you probably wanted to. And thanks for the tech support. And I'm grateful for your willingness to visit obscure places with me.

Chris Minato, thanks for being a fellow ghost enthusiast (and being willing to talk about it!) and letting me lean on your cultural expertise and family experience. And thanks for riding the light rail with me—the scariest experience of all—when we were both at SJSU.

Bobbi Arduini, thanks for letting me be your paranormal pathfinder, and thanks for your pathfinding on our hikes.

Mike Espinoza, I greatly appreciate your patience in tolerating my questions that you couldn't possibly have had the answers to and your consistent, quiet encouragement.

Jeff Bengford and Kellye Dodd, thank you for insightful conversations and the behind-the-scenes tour.

Niki Hinds and Suzy Brooks, thank you for your research assistance and for being marvelous colleagues and friends.

I appreciate the assistance from Shane Curtin and Michael at the California Room of the Dr. Martin Luther King Jr. Library and also from Kitty Monahan.

INTRODUCTION

Long before San Jose and the surrounding areas were known as Silicon Valley, or even the Valley of Heart's Delight, they were the ancestral home of the Ohlone people. The Ohlone comprised a number of Native American groups that occupied the lands from northeast of the San Francisco Bay to south of Monterey Bay. Eventually, many of these groups were enfolded into the Spanish mission system, where their beliefs and customs were subsumed by those of European Catholicism. But the Ohlone had their own long and rich heritage of beliefs and rituals, including views and customs surrounding death and the afterlife.

The Ohlone people believed the dead went to a "land across the sea." After death, the bodies were buried or cremated, their belongings interred or burned with them, and the dead were not spoken of again. The ceremonies of death, which had to be carried out precisely, were in aid of speeding the spirit of the deceased to the Island of the Dead, where they would be received by other spirits. The family members of the departed practiced caution. After all, while the body may have been disposed of, the soul may not yet have completed its journey to the other world. Family members feared that in its loneliness the ghost of the deceased might be drawn back to its possessions or relatives. For this reason, as well as from grief, a person's dwelling and belongings were destroyed after death.

In addition, the widow of a dead man would disguise her face with ash and singe her hair so as not to be recognized by her husband's ghost, which was said to walk among his people shortly after death and before his departure to the afterlife. The spirit would be angered if the ceremonies were not properly held. The threat of a ghost remaining on earth, among his loved ones and possessions, was a real one for the Ohlone people.

But what about today? In our land of high-tech science and modern thought, surely we don't harbor the same beliefs that the souls of the dead might remain earthbound or even cause harm to those still living. Or do we?

As we can see from the Ohlone assurance of life after death, belief in ghosts transcends time and culture. Many people today are just as likely to believe in ghosts or spirits as our ancestors were. The concept of what a ghost is hasn't changed much, either. The word itself dates to about 2500 BC, when a proto–Indo European root, *gheis*, formed words related to excitement, amazement and fear. This in turn evolved into the Old English word *gast*, used for the spirit or soul of a dead person, especially one that appears to the living. This is very much how people define the term today, though the way in which a ghost might present itself changes with the times. The ghost of yesteryear, limited to communicating through raps on a wall, can now manipulate sophisticated electronic devices, much to the excitement of television ghost hunters everywhere.

However they manifest, the spirits of the dead haunt every corner of San Jose today, appearing to those willing to see them and those who would prefer not to. The ghosts of San Jose continue to inspire excitement, amazement and fear, and their stories make up an important layer of the city's history, connecting our present to our past.

1
LOCAL LANDMARKS

HAYES MANSION

On the edge of south San Jose, in the Edenvale neighborhood, nestled on a plot of land adjoining what is now Edenvale Gardens Regional Park, sits the large hotel-and-conference-venue complex known familiarly as the Hayes Mansion. The beautifully crafted home contains imported marbles, exotic woods and fire-safety features not often seen in a building of its time, such as metal doors and fire-hose cabinets throughout. The red-tiled-roof building, constructed in the form of a Maltese cross, has a long center section containing a solarium that connects the north and south wings and a loggia that connects the east and west wings. Mature palm trees surrounding the house provide a tropical counterpart to the native oaks skirting the perimeter. The property is currently owned by a real estate investment firm and operated as a resort under the name of a famous upscale hotel chain. Throughout its history as a hotel, it's been a popular location for a range of clients, from honeymooning couples to Silicon Valley tech executives. But the mansion's history predates the modern expansion of the valley and is more bizarre than meets the eye.

In 1887, matriarch Mary Hayes-Chynoweth, born Mary Folsom and twice widowed, moved to San Jose with her two grown sons, Jay O. and Everis A. Hayes, after making a family fortune mining in Wisconsin and Michigan. The first house they built on the 239-acre property, in 1891,

Mary Hayes Chynoweth never got to see the completed Spanish Colonial Revival house that we now know as the Hayes Mansion. *Author photo.*

burned to the ground eight years later. Construction on the Spanish Colonial Revival house that we now know as the Hayes Mansion began in 1903; it was completed in late 1905. Unfortunately, Mrs. Hayes-Chynoweth passed away earlier that year and never got to see the finished home. The house, at forty-one thousand square feet with sixty-four rooms, was built to accommodate three families. After Mary's death, her sons and their families moved in. During their tenure in the home, both brothers were involved in state and national politics, continued to own and operate mines and purchased three local newspapers, which eventually became the *San Jose Mercury News*. They occupied the home until 1954 (some sources say 1952), when they sold it to a private buyer, along with parkland north of the house that was turned into the Frontier Village amusement park. In 1975, the house was listed in the National Register of Historical Places, and ten years later, the City of San Jose purchased the home, the park area and the remaining adjoining land and eventually turned the mansion into a conference center. After several failed attempts by the city at offloading the property, which cost taxpayers millions of dollars in operating costs after its projected revenue failed to materialize, the house and land are once again privately owned.

The original Hayes estate was completely self-sustaining, operating as its own little town with orchards and gardens, a post office and a railroad station, as well as a chapel built by Mary Hayes-Chynoweth. It was also the site where Mrs. Hayes-Chynoweth practiced her longtime interest in faith healing and spiritualism, which is where our ghostly tales have their origin. Before moving to California, she was well known in her home state of Wisconsin as a religious mystic. She denounced the traditional practices of Spiritualism, a movement that was sweeping the nation in the mid-nineteenth century, as hoaxes or distractions. She focused not on table rapping or séances but instead on what she viewed as God-given powers within her. She told her biographer of the first experience she had with these powers, in 1853, when she was a young schoolteacher: "I was crossing the kitchen with a basin of water when, suddenly, some unknown Force pressed me down upon my knees, helpless.…Of my own will I could not move nor see nor speak; but a compelling Power moved my tongue to prayer in language or languages unknown to me." According to this invisible "Force," she should spend the rest of her life in service to others, using her newly discovered powers for healing through spiritual medicine.

What Hayes-Chynoweth called "the Power" allowed her to see through the human body and thus pinpoint locations and causes of diseases and ailments. Her practice as a healer was to use the laying-on of hands to take another person's symptoms into her own body, causing her to break out in the same rashes, tumors or pains that had plagued the person. The suffering person in turn recovered. She used prayer and meditation for patience in enduring these discomforts and illnesses and for guidance on prescribing herbs, nutrition and other remedies to speed people on the path to recovery. Even before her experience with the "Force," she possessed some innate knowledge of healing. As a five-year-old child, she soothed her younger sister who was suffering from burns. As a ten-year-old, without any knowledge of or training in herbal remedies, she administered angelica tea to a woman who was thought to be dead, reviving the woman and earning the praise of an arriving physician.

After coming into her "Power" and teaching herself how to harness her gift, she began traveling from town to town, preaching and healing. She found popularity and gratitude among those who availed themselves of her services but rarely took payment for her spiritual intervention unless pressed. And, in those instances, she used her earnings to support her parents and pay off the mortgage on their farm. She preferred to present herself simply as a medium or conduit, sharing her gift from God for the benefit of others. Sometimes, though, she did use her gift for her own benefit.

In addition to her ability to heal, Hayes-Chynoweth could speak in languages she claimed not to know and could see into the future, correctly predicting unexpected visitors, economic trends and market prices. This allowed her to offer advice to her sons on investments and financial management. In 1882, her Power guided her and her sons to invest in profitable mining land in Wisconsin, which is where they made the fortune that enabled them to move west to California, live comfortably and build extravagantly.

Hayes-Chynoweth continued to refer to her estate as Edenvale, as the original owners, the Tennants, had done. In addition to commissioning the Mediterranean-style mansion to replace the original Queen Anne Victorian that burned, she built the Sandstone Chapel and established the True Life Church of San Jose, serving as pastor of the church until her death and publishing a monthly pamphlet with her teachings.

Though she was unable to save from death her two husbands and her youngest son, who died as a toddler, stories of Hayes-Chynoweth's healing prowess abound, and the popularity she enjoyed earlier in her life as a traveling preacher renewed itself among the people of San Jose. In the 1890s, she received well over three thousand visitors a year at her home in Edenvale, most suffering from illnesses doctors had deemed incurable. Contemporary eyewitnesses to her rituals of healing spoke of "cancerous tumors moved from patients' bodies to her own, cripples [who] threw away their crutches and danced on the lawn and the terminally ill [who] went on to live for decades." In an unverified story, she even knew that her daughter-in-law would suffer not from pregnancy, as the daughter-in-law thought, but from tumors in her abdomen.

Hayes Home Edenvale, near San Jose, Cal.

The Hayes Mansion, circa 1905–10, when it was still a private residence. *Hayes Mansion, Edenvale. Courtesy of San Jose Public Library, California Room, Historic Postcard Collection.*

Most stories today of paranormal activity at the Hayes Mansion are vague and imprecise, yet many people agree, without even knowing much about its matriarch, that the house is haunted. People report a sensation of being watched as they wander through the halls that are part of the original mansion. One rumor is that late at night the sounds of children playing in the hallways can be heard, and several guests have reported seeing a child riding a tricycle, even when no children are staying at the hotel. Another story mentions the spirit of a man who may be a caretaker or someone who looked after the house during its period of neglect in the 1960s. Few witnesses, however, claim this specific sighting. Lingering feelings of unease and dread follow people throughout the building, which may stem from its use as an alcohol rehabilitation center before its restoration.

A couple who tried to stay overnight at the hotel in 2005 shared with me an unforgettable experience. As soon as Danny Diaz and his wife checked in, they started experiencing alarming feelings of being watched, the same sensation reported by many others. Assured by the desk clerk that the room they were staying in was a new addition to the building and not part of the Hayes's home, they attempted to relax in their room, but the feelings of unease and dread continued.

They finally managed to fall asleep but around 3:00 a.m. were abruptly awakened by a loud noise in their room. Jumping out of bed to investigate, Danny discovered that a light bulb in the bathroom had suddenly and inexplicably fallen from the ceiling and shattered. But instead of breaking into glass shards, it was pulverized into a fine dust.

The maintenance man sent by the front desk to clean up the mess didn't offer the Diazes any reassurance. "He looked nervous," Danny said. "His hands were shaking. We asked him if he knew anything about the place being haunted." He believed in bad spirits, the man told the couple, and when something happened that could hurt someone, such as the falling light bulb, it was a bad spirit. They should leave at once.

The man's ominous advice so moved the couple that they packed their belongings and left in the middle of the night. But the unsettling feelings did not dissipate immediately. Danny remembers feeling that they were being watched as they walked to the parking lot, and his wife agreed. "We looked back and it was all dark," he said, but they knew something "wasn't right." Considering the long legacy of the house, it could have been any number of spirits that threatened the couple.

Mary Hayes-Chynoweth's last words were, "I have never wronged anyone," a mysterious utterance from a woman who devoted her life to physical healing and spiritual leadership. Was it a statement of contentment on a life well lived? Or was it too much of a protest, aimed at convincing those who would naysay her power? The manifestation of latent guilt for those she could not save? We'll never know what she meant or whether her power existed outside of her own head, but the legacy she leaves is an impressive lesson in faith.

Winchester Mystery House®

Without a doubt, the most famous haunted location in San Jose and the South Bay is the Winchester Mystery House®. Indeed, it may be the most famous tourist attraction—haunted or not—in the entire city, and paranormal enthusiasts from across the nation who know nothing else about California's third-largest city at least know of this house.

The history of the woman who built the house has taken on legendary status, but the "facts," as they're reported, have been conflated with fiction. We do know that Sarah Pardee was born about 1839 in New Haven, Connecticut, and in 1862 married William Wirt Winchester. William's father had established the Winchester Repeating Arms Company, which became immensely successful from the manufacture of firearms such as the Winchester Model 1873 rifle, which would become known as "the gun that won the West." In 1866, Sarah experienced the first of her personal tragedies when her infant daughter, Annie, died. Fifteen years later, her husband died after a long illness; as his widow, Sarah inherited a 50 percent share in the Winchester company, worth approximately $20 million at the time ($500 million today).

In 1886, Sarah followed her sister across the country to San Jose and purchased an eight-room farmhouse on forty acres of land. Over the next twenty years, she expanded the house at a total cost of $5 million ($71 million today). Of course, as heir to the Winchester Repeating Arms Company, this was a cost she could easily bear. Various sources report that her daily income from the company was over $1,000 ($25,000 in today's terms). She used her wealth not only to make the house massive but also to beautify it, installing windows, chandeliers and other works of stained glass made by John Mallon and having furniture and trim custom-built to her specifications. Some sources of the time reported that she kept the construction ongoing, around the clock, 365 days a year, until her death in 1922. While this claim

The front of the Winchester house, San Jose's most famous landmark. *Author photo.*

adds a tidbit of eccentricity to Sarah's character, it is disproved by her own documentation from the time. A letter to her sister states that she gave her workers time off during the winter. However, the size and scope of the house today is evidence that construction clearly was a vast undertaking.

Just how large is Sarah Winchester's house? The Winchester Mystery House® website reports that it is more than 24,000 square feet and contains "10,000 windows, 2,000 doors, 160 rooms, 52 skylights, 47 stairways and fireplaces, 17 chimneys, 13 bathrooms, 6 kitchens." Some of the more unusual features of the house—those that put the "mystery" in its name and are emphasized on the tour—include doors and windows to nowhere, a staircase that ends at the ceiling and a small room in the center of the house with two doorways, one leading in and one leading out.

This puzzling room, called by tour guides the "séance room," is at the literal and metaphorical heart of the mysterious house. Why on earth would Sarah Winchester need such an inaccessible room, and what do séances have to do with it?

In this room, with one entrance and one exit, it's said that Sarah communicated with spirits of the dead. Sitting here in the blackness of night, between 1:00 and 2:00 a.m., she would receive the building plans she

The Winchester house features custom windows, woodwork and furniture. *Author photo*.

needed to keep constructing the mansion—construction, she believed, that would protect her from the spirits that had followed her from her home in Connecticut and were possibly responsible for the deaths of her child and husband.

After her husband's death in 1881, it's rumored that Sarah Winchester visited a famous Boston psychic medium, Adam Coons, who told her that

The Winchester house before the 1906 earthquake. The earthquake caused the central tower to collapse into the floors below; it was never rebuilt. *Winchester Mystery House before the 1906 Earthquake. Courtesy of San Jose Public Library, California Room, Historic Postcard Collection.*

her family was cursed and that she was destined to be tormented by all the souls of people killed by Winchester rifles. To keep the spirits at bay, she must build a house that would confuse and entrap these vengeful spirits. And as long as construction continued, she would be protected from an otherworldly assault. (While it's likely that Sarah explored the then-popular field of Spiritualism, no record has been found of her visiting the psychic or even that Coons was practicing in Boston at the time of her alleged conference with him.) Thus begins the legend of Sarah's supposed obsession with building: a mortal fear of the spirits she believed were pursuing her and a feverish desire to outsmart them. When construction ended, she believed, she would die.

In addition to spirits of those murdered by Winchester rifles, including Native Americans killed by white settlers, the house is rumored to be haunted by workers who never left, ghosts responsible for the 1906 earthquake (which caused Sarah to close up a room to try to trap them) and possibly even Sarah herself. The apparition reported most often by witnesses is of a man wearing overalls and a cap roaming the property, including the interior of the house. He's been dubbed "Clyde" by employees and is thought to be a former caretaker, still performing his duties a century after his employer's death. The other apparition sometimes seen is that of a petite, gray-haired woman. People believe this to be the spectral mistress of the house.

Other unexplained phenomena include shadow figures moving along dark corridors inside the home, the visible impression of someone lying on Sarah's bed in the room where she died, palpable cold spots appearing from nowhere, rocking chairs moving, doorknobs turning on their own and the disembodied sounds of people talking and laughing in rooms that are empty. Glowing lights and orbs are not uncommon, as are doors opening and closing by themselves.

A former manager at the house experienced some typical activity. Allen Weitzel was responsible for closing up the house after the last tours of the day. Once all the guests and other employees were gone, he did a final walk-through of the house, securing doors and shutting off lights in each room as he left it. In the gift shop, he set the alarm and exited to the parking lot. Once outside, he glanced up to make sure the house was dark for the night. It was. A short walk brought him to his car, where he looked up at the house one more time as he prepared to drive away. This time, as he watched, all the lights on the third floor flickered to life.

A tour guide at the house told me that he was alone on the third floor when he heard footsteps near him. He looked out a nearby door to an exterior portion of the house and saw a figure a few feet away. Assuming it was another employee or a guest, he decided to greet the person. But as he approached, he remembered that the house was not currently open for tours, and all at once the figure slowly disappeared in front of him. There were no other employees or guides in that area of the house at all.

I've had my own experience at the Winchester Mystery House® that I could not explain. Many years ago, I was on a behind-the-scenes tour that visited areas not included on the standard mansion tour, including the basement. Our small group of eight or so people, plus the tour guide, donned hard hats and ventured down a short flight of steps, accessed from a set of doors inside the house near the carriage entrance. Under the house, light filtered in dimly through windows set high in the walls, revealing pipes and ducts and cramped storage spaces. There was enough light to see by, but the guide had a flashlight, which she kept aimed near the floor to help us find our footing.

As we were standing in one of the larger rooms of the basement, the guide, facing us, with her flashlight turned off and hanging loosely in her hand, responded to a question about ghost sightings in the basement. She mentioned the apparition of the overalls-clad workman who has frequently been spotted in the area. As she spoke, I saw a circle of light bouncing along one of the walls, up near the ceiling, about twenty feet behind her. It was above the windows, so it couldn't have been light coming in through a window. Turning to look behind me, I saw no light source that could explain the moving circle I was seeing. I turned to my friend. "Do you see that?," I murmured. She had already spotted it and nodded, her eyes tracking the circle of light as it bounced for a second along the top of the wall, then disappeared.

Was it paranormal? I can't say for sure, but considering that other baffling activity in the house involves lights and illumination, it seems possible. A quick survey of my surroundings didn't reveal any natural explanation, and it did occur in an area of the house where other sightings have been reported. It could have been the workman, or it could have been someone else entirely. Perhaps it was the energy of Sarah Winchester herself, returning to keep an eye on the strangers prowling through her home.

The ghost stories are entertaining, without a doubt. However, the truth of Sarah Winchester's life, while a little less spooky, is fascinating in its own right. According to local professor and historian Mary Jo Ignoffo in her book *The Captive of the Labyrinth*, Sarah was actually a woman ahead of her time: an architect when it wasn't a profession available to women and a philanthropist who preferred to make her contributions anonymously in an era when the wealthy were expected to give away their money publicly and ostentatiously. Many of the oddities in the house are easily explained with some critical assessment: as a self-taught architect, Winchester experimented with design through trial and error on her own home, reconfiguring a room or passageway if the lighting was poor, moving an entrance to a room to improve flow through the house and removing a second-floor balcony but leaving the "doorway to nowhere." A bell tower on the roof collapsed into the floors below it during the 1906 earthquake, and Winchester simply boarded over the destruction rather than rebuild, leaving the stairway to the ceiling. Details of the house considered eerie, such as sink drains with thirteen holes, were added after Winchester's death by the amusement company that leased the house in order to play up her ostensible obsession with the number thirteen (which was never recorded anywhere in contemporary writings about Winchester). As for the séance room? There are no reports of Winchester holding a séance in the house or anywhere else. In his book *Ghostland*, author Colin Dickey asserts that it was her gardener's bedroom.

The stories that swirled around her probably stemmed from criticisms of the private, retiring life she led. And these stories, fueled by clever marketing aimed at luring paying visitors to the home as a tourist attraction, evolved into the legends we know today. But even as we finally acknowledge Sarah Winchester for her philanthropic and architectural contributions, we can continue to recognize how her life has contributed to the mythology and lore of San Jose. It's possible for these two ideas to coexist: Winchester could be misunderstood and misinterpreted, *and* ghosts could be present in the house. The two don't have to be mutually exclusive, and my own experience—and that of countless others who have witnessed extraordinary things at the house—points to the possibility that there may be some facts in the fiction after all.

CHUCK E. CHEESE

Chuck E. Cheese's pervasive advertising jingle proclaims that the entertainment venues are "where a kid can be a kid." For at least one unfortunate soul, what is arguably the most famous Chuck E. Cheese location in the nation ended up being where a kid can be a ghost.

It may come as a surprise to generations of San Joseans who grew up attending birthday parties at various Chuck E. Cheese locations throughout town, but the chain got its start as Chuck E. Cheese's Pizza Time Theater in San Jose in 1977, with its original location on South Winchester Boulevard. The site of the Chuck E. Cheese at 2445 Fontaine Road, more commonly referred to as the Tully Road location, is where children can win tickets from arcade games, have fun on mechanical rides, run wild in play zones, watch stage shows featuring performers costumed as animals (the animatronics are now retired) and eat pizza to their hearts' content. Its most noteworthy feature is the thirty-foot-tall statue of Mr. Cheese himself, displayed in the window alcove and visible from Highway 101. An equally popular aspect of this location that appeals less to children and more to paranormal enthusiasts is its haunted reputation.

One story that has circulated from its inception is that shortly after the location opened, a family with a three-year-old child arrived to enjoy the fun and games on offer. When the mother went off to the restroom, her young son went looking for her, climbing the stairs to the second floor. He saw her exit the restroom on the floor below and tried to run downstairs to her but tripped and fell all the way to the bottom of the stairs, breaking his neck. Employees who share this story claim the boy's spirit operates one of the rides at closing time, when all the machines should be powered off. They also say you can hear him throughout the building, calling for his mother.

Another story that is often accepted as the truth behind the haunting is that of a young girl who fell to her death from either an interior balcony on the third floor or from a third-floor window to the parking lot below. It's not known whether this happened when the building was previously occupied or during its tenure as Chuck E. Cheese, but the girl has been seen by employees on the third floor as well as by people outside the building who look back from the parking lot and see her face peering out of an upper window. Employees who have access to the storage area on the third floor report feelings of unease, physical discomfort such as headaches, the sounds of children at play even after the facility is closed for the night and perpetually malfunctioning lights that leave one corner of the space in darkness.

The thirty-foot-tall Chuck E. Cheese is the last of three statues that welcomed visitors to the location off Tully Road. *Author photo.*

The history of the building seems to disprove the possibility of any previously living spirit. Before it was Chuck E. Cheese, it was the Magic Village Toy Shop. Those of a certain age fondly remember three giant toy soldiers in the windows. (Many people erroneously remember the building as home to King Norman's Kingdom of Toys, but a 1978 issue of the *Spartan*

Daily newspaper confirms that King Norman's was located in Eastridge Mall.) No documentation exists that any deaths occurred at the property on Fontaine Road at any time, but some people remember hearing rumors that the building was haunted when it was still a toy store. Paranormal investigator Nick Groff has a theory about the ghost girl, which he shared in an interview with the San Jose Inside website. "It could be somewhat like a tulpa—thought-form energy," he said. In the paranormal field, a tulpa (a term borrowed from Tibetan Buddhism) is a being that is brought to life by drawing on energy from the collective thoughts that surround it, something make-believe that becomes tangible through the force of the imagination. Groff says: "People have had experiences, thought it was a little girl, and over time it manifested as a little girl. I believe something like that could have happened at Chuck E. Cheese, but I don't know." If enough people walk into the building expecting to see the ghost of a little girl and project that mental energy into the space, eventually, that energy might coalesce into something that other people can experience.

Could this explain what so many people claim to see in the third-floor window? Could it also be the basis of the poor little boy calling for his mother? Possibly, and without any verified deaths on the premises, it seems more than likely that the power of thought has brought the spirit into existence. Whether the ghost at Tully and Fontaine is an organic spirit or one conjured by pizza-fueled masses, it's now part of the legacy of one of San Jose's proudest institutions.

KELLEY PARK / HAPPY HOLLOW

One of San Jose's most beloved diversions for families and animal lovers is—incredibly—haunted. It seems far-fetched, but rumors and stories have been swirling around Happy Hollow Park and Zoo and Kelley Park for decades.

Kelley Park, on Senter Road, is a centrally located city park containing the Japanese Friendship Garden, Happy Hollow, History Park and open spaces for picnics and playing. The 160-acre property was purchased in 1861 by Judge Lawrence Archer, a prominent county judge, state legislator and two-term city mayor who moved his family there in 1869. The land was planted extensively with luscious fruit trees, including a cherry orchard of which Judge Archer was particularly proud. His only daughter, Louise Archer Flavin Kelley, inherited the property in 1910 and built a home there in 1912. When Louise's health began to fail, she put up a portion of her estate for sale. It was purchased by the City of San Jose for preservation as a park. A condition of the sale was that Mrs. Kelley would be allowed to remain in her home for the rest of her days, and so she did, passing away in February 1952. Learning that her family's acreage would be preserved as a park, she had hoped it would be named Archer Park, after her father. Instead, it was christened Kelley Park, after her married name.

Happy Hollow was the first attraction opened at the park, in 1961. The Japanese Friendship Garden, built to honor San Jose's sister city of Okayama, Japan, opened in 1965. History Park, a collection of original and replica historical buildings and landmarks that functions as a living museum, opened in 1971.

The Kelley House, where Louise Archer Kelley lived until her death, was a 5,200-square-foot, two-story home visible along the path to Happy Hollow's current entrance from the west parking lot. It was destined for the National Register of Historic Places. According to the Preliminary Historic Architectural Evaluation, prepared in 1994 at the request of the city in anticipation of a proposed expansion of Kelley Park: "The house represents a particularly unique combination of residential styles—Craftsman bungalow, Prairie School and Classical Revival—popular during the first decade of this century. In its massing, scale, and ornamental details…the Kelley House can certainly be identified as domestic design that is more distinguished than the typical house from this period. The house has only received minor alterations since it was originally built, and thus it retains a high level of integrity."

This assessment makes the home's fate all the more heartbreaking. In 2012, it was heavily damaged in a fire and had to be demolished, though the carriage house remains. Before its demise, the house was the setting of the primary ghost story of Kelley Park. Passersby, many of whom were in the park at dusk, reported gazing at the house and being startled to see the pale, luminous face of a woman staring back at them from second-floor windows—this before the home's use as living quarters for park rangers. When looked at more closely, the spectral face would vanish, leaving witnesses wondering if they had caught an illicit glance into the past or if one of its previous occupants had never left. We will never again be able to witness the face in the window ourselves. But thanks to modern technology and a partnership between History San José and Virtual Design Analysis Group, a three-dimensional digital scan of the house was conducted before its charred remnants were removed. Via a video available online, we can step inside the postfire remains of the home.

Viewing the carnage from the fire, the once-beautiful home takes on a sinister appearance, and it's easy to believe a darker force was at play in its fiery destruction. Large living rooms, opening symmetrically off a central hall, are littered with fallen wooden beams, partially incinerated, and huge holes gape through the plaster and lath on the walls. The doors to built-in cabinets have fallen or burned away, revealing lines of shelves standing forlornly empty. Upstairs, a pair of double doors opens to a balcony that has fallen through to the front porch below, and the ceiling is open to the heavens through a roof that has burned to the point of collapse. Louise Archer Kelley would have been most distressed to see the remains of her home. But perhaps she, or the woman in the window, was not confined by the stucco walls and now roams the grounds of the park, biding her time until she appears to onlookers again. Perhaps it's just a matter of time before a new ghost story comes to life.

Kelley House was once the most historic attraction in the park. The most treasured feature is Happy Hollow, a sixteen-acre, family-oriented amusement park and zoo that also offers programs for wildlife conservation and education. Inspired by the 1955 opening of Disneyland in Anaheim, San Jose city leaders purchased seven and a half acres on the edge of Kelley Park and began planning the amusement park at Happy Hollow, which opened on March 27, 1961. In its early years, it featured rides relocated from Alum Rock Park as well as one of its most enduring and beloved attractions, the Danny the Dragon train ride. The Zoo in the Hollow, on the east side of the amusement area, was added later in the decade, and the park became an accredited zoo in 1993, which it remains today. A two-year renovation added the restaurant, gift shop and education center and resulted in the property as we know it today. The refurbishment didn't deter the ghosts that are said to have existed there for years—perhaps it stirred up new ones.

One of the most disturbing stories comes from an online source that reports that, at closing time one evening, an employee was checking the property for errant visitors. Spotting a teenage boy at one of the exhibits in the zoo area, the employee called out that the park was now closed, but as the man approached, the boy whirled to face him and, screaming, lifted his own head from his body. Unfortunately, that's where the story ends, and we have no information about the employee's reaction (or continued employment at the park) or if the headless boy was ever seen again.

A more persistent myth involves the tale of a young woman whose murdered body was left in Coyote Creek, on the other side of the fence that runs along Happy Hollow's property line. The apparition of this woman has

The entrance plaza to Happy Hollow Park and Zoo in Kelley Park. *Author photo*.

been reported multiple times, wandering along the fence and sometimes in the creek. She always wears a short red dress with a black belt and has long black hair that obscures her face. Some people say that if you go down to the creek behind the park around midnight and call out the name "Christy," the ghost of the woman will appear. The story claims that the woman died in the 1970s, but in 2003, a young woman's body was found along the creek bank in this area. Her unsolved murder is one of the San Jose Police Department's cold cases. This sad event is just one instance of tragedy in an area—along the creek from Kelley Park to the north side of Story Road—that has long been troubled. For many years, it was the site of a large, semipermanent homeless encampment known as the "Jungle," where crime and even deaths occurred frequently. Surely some of that energy of despair, tragedy and trauma has made an imprint on the land, resulting in the manifestation of restless spirits with nowhere else to go.

Happy Hollow and the other attractions in Kelley Park continue to be beloved destinations for families, residents and other visitors. The delighted laughter of children and tranquil conversation of adults can be heard echoing throughout the park. The stories shouldn't deter anyone from visiting, but they should encourage guests to keep their eyes open. They, too, might witness a vision from darker times past.

2
SCHOOLS

ARBUCKLE ELEMENTARY

The fantastically named Cinderella Lane on the east side of San Jose seems like it would be the setting for a fairy tale, but the story that's told about Clyde Arbuckle Elementary School is not fit for the ears of children. The campus now houses Adelante II Academy but was for many years the home of Arbuckle Elementary, named after a prominent local historian to whom we owe much of our guardianship of San Jose's historical artifacts. According to History San José, the society he helped found, Arbuckle, born in 1903, was from a pioneer family and was "widely considered an authority on local history." Appointed to the honorary position of city historian, he became a collector and preservationist of documents and objects from San Jose's early days that eventually wound up as part of the State House Museum, of which Arbuckle was also director and curator. This became the San Jose Historical Museum (now History San José), which, thanks in large part to Arbuckle's tireless work, safeguards an impressive collection of regional history, the largest in the state of California.

The school that bears Clyde Arbuckle's name is in a neighborhood that has its own tale to tell. Story Road was named after the homestead of Alanson Story (sometimes spelled Alonson), who in 1851 established the first farm in the area, south of where Highway 680 runs today. Nearly a century later, when developers built the subdivision that now occupies the land

The Arbuckle Children's Center is located on the magically named Cinderella Lane. *Author photo.*

northeast of the Story and King Roads intersection, they seem to have been inspired by Mr. Story's name, christening the streets in the development after works of fiction. A perusal of a map of this area is a delight. In addition to Cinderella Lane, there's Tiara Drive and Diadem Drive (accessories fit for a princess). Cinderella intersects with Peter Pan Avenue, which turns into Van Winkle Lane and crosses Galahad and Sinbad Avenues and Lilliput Lane. One block north is Bambi Avenue, and one block south, Sleepy Hollow Lane turns into Cotton Tail Avenue.

Unfortunately for those hoping for a fairy-tale ending, the legend attached to the school is more along the lines of the Brothers Grimm than Disney. In the 1970s, it's said in an oft-repeated story, a boy was murdered on the school grounds, being brutally stabbed multiple times in the back. In recent decades, those living in the neighborhood and people driving by the school at night have reported seeing the ghastly ghost of the boy on campus, a distinct apparition that roams between buildings and over the playing fields. Some even say if you're brave enough to get close, you can see the bloody knife protruding from the dead boy's back.

The history of the land, and the idea of a murdered boy remaining tethered to the place of his untimely death, is captivating. But there's a problem with this story. Clyde Arbuckle Elementary School didn't open until 1980, and there are no records of deaths associated with the property. However, there is a documented murder that occurred in 1996 at Clyde L. Fischer Middle School, a mile south of Arbuckle Elementary on Hopkins Drive. News reports state that on the field behind the school, a twenty-four-year-old man got into an argument with a fourteen-year-old boy and fatally stabbed the boy—in the back. Strangely enough, there are no ghost stories associated with Fischer Middle School, so the logical explanation is that the story has become confused after repeated tellings of the legend, and the two schools named after Clydes have been conflated. But is it possible one of them really is haunted? Have people really seen the ghost of a murdered boy, and is that why the legend has persisted after all these years? Perhaps the only way to find out is to visit on your own. Or maybe it's time to put this tragic true-crime story—and its poor young victim—to rest.

BERNAL INTERMEDIATE

Bernal Intermediate School, a junior high school in the Rancho Santa Teresa neighborhood, opened in 1980, but the history of the land it was built on dates back more than three thousand years. The Muwekma Ohlone Indians, the original inhabitants of the land, used this area as a village and permanent burial ground due to its proximity to a freshwater source at Santa Teresa Springs, known now as Dottie's Pond. In 1826, José Joaquin Bernal, a retired Spanish soldier, acquired this parcel of land, which he called Rancho Santa Teresa, as a land grant from the Mexican government after passing through as a member of the de Anza expedition. José Bernal's grandson, Ygnacio Bernal, built the adobe house that originally stood adjacent to the school on land that now comprises part of Santa Teresa County Park.

The perimeter of Bernal Intermediate's playing fields edges what used to be a prehistoric burial mound, used by the Ohlone people. It is the location of at least twenty recorded graves. According to Michael Boulland, a local historian who writes about this area in his booklet "Whoppers and Ghostly Tales from Rancho Santa Teresa," at some point before 1973, utility crews excavating near the site discovered ancient human remains. This led to an archaeological investigation that uncovered a prehistoric village, including

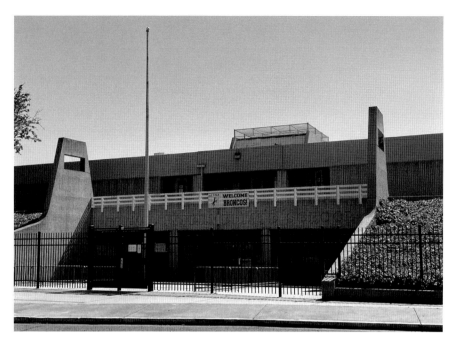

Bernal Intermediate School is located on the site of a Muwekma Ohlone burial mound. *Author photo.*

this newly uncovered permanent burial site. Before the City of San Jose would issue building permits to the Oak Grove School District for a new intermediate school, it required confirmation that any human remains were properly removed and relocated. Likewise, the district was eager to ensure that it would not be building a school on top of dead bodies.

Those who originally lived and were interred on the land may be responsible for the variety of spectral activity at Bernal Intermediate, or perhaps it is related to the era of Mexican occupation.

Boulland relates the experiences of a former custodian at the school who found himself regularly working alone as darkness fell on campus. The custodian was vacuuming on the second floor when he felt another presence in the hall with him. He looked up and saw, about ten feet away, the figure of a "beautiful, strangely dressed Spanish woman" in her early twenties wearing a long, dark, Victorian-style dress. On her wrists, instead of sleeves, she had white lace bands, and her dark hair was coiled up in a bun held with a black comb.

The vision gave him chills, the custodian reported to Boulland, and his heart pounded as the woman floated toward him, seemingly without using her feet. She moved past him, never once looking back, and disappeared down the hall as she approached the elevator. An alarmed telephone call to his supervisor resulted in the supervisor instructing him to call the police, but the custodian wondered, as many of us would, "How does someone report seeing a ghost to the police?"

He wasn't frightened to continue working at the school, not even when he was alone at night, and he never saw the apparition of the woman again. However, his story took on a life of its own, demonstrating just how fallible and unreliable—yet creative—the oral tradition can be.

In the retelling of this story, whether by staff or students at the school or maybe even those outside the community, the ghost undergoes a drastic change. Alternate versions of the story report that the custodian frequently saw the spirit of a man with a large wart on the end of his nose who appeared in various places on the upper floor of the building during the night shift. In these renditions, the custodian drew sketches of the spirit he saw, always illustrating the same man, and he seemed fearful of the ghost, sometimes hesitating to perform his custodial tasks on the second floor. People who claim to have seen or owned copies of the sketches are unable to produce them, and this retelling obviously differs greatly from the custodian's own account.

Then there are stories from another employee of the school that also cannot be confirmed or denied. According to Boulland, at a later point in time than the original sighting of the Spanish woman, another custodian had his own strange experiences on the second floor, specifically with an elevator that seemed to have an uncanny mind of its own. While working into the evening hours, when all the teachers and students had gone home for the day and when he knew he was alone in the building, this custodian would hear the elevator come to life. He heard the banging of the motor and the whirring as it traveled between floors. What was even more alarming to him was that the elevator could only be operated by a key, to prevent students from using it. And he knew that at that time of night, he was the only one who had the key.

Boulland claims that the two custodians worked at the school at different times and didn't know each other, and that the latter had heard no reports of alleged activity on the site. Even more eerie is that the first custodian, the one who saw the beautiful young woman, reported seeing her upstairs in the vicinity of the elevator.

Other reports of strange and possibly paranormal activity at the school include a bottle of paint exploding inside a locked closet—a closet that backed up to the elevator hallway, lights in the performing arts room flickering on and off with no explanation and voices coming from empty classrooms. Boulland also writes of being informed by a teacher at the school about the death of a homeless man outside one of the classrooms. His spiritual energy might linger and be another factor in the school's haunting.

With such prolific otherworldly activity, it's no wonder that both teachers and students are enthusiastic about spreading—and possibly altering—the legends of the school. So much of what is shared is rumor and conjecture, and yet the ghost stories have such an air of authenticity and earnestness that it's hard not to believe they are true. The very land in this neighborhood around the Santa Teresa hills seems to pulsate with history and energy. The custodian's story leaves little doubt that these echoes of the past have seeped into the hallways of Bernal Intermediate.

DEL MAR HIGH

Del Mar High School, on the west side of San Jose near the Campbell border, sits on a triangular plot of land. The front of the school faces Del Mar Avenue, a nondescript street lined with chain-link fences and parking lots. But it's the section of the school tucked away in the back, along Southwest Expressway, that commands the attention of ghost hunters and sends chills down the spines of those students brave enough to venture onto campus at night, where a decades-old ghost still roams.

The school opened in 1959. Seventeen years before, in 1942, the ground that the school stands on was covered in fruit orchards, like much of the rest of the valley. Legend has it that, on the plot of land where the football field is today, a boy was murdered by his best friend. Witnesses who have been on school grounds in the middle of the night say that if you listen carefully, at 3:15 a.m., the time the murder was supposed to have occurred, you can hear a boy screaming for help, his cries echoing across what are now the athletic fields. Some even claim to have seen an indistinct yet unmistakably human figure running up and down the bleachers at the football field in the middle of the night, when no earthly person has business being there. In addition, the area of campus nearest the football bowl draws ominous visitors: a murder of crows. The birds perch on nearby buildings and make an unearthly, portentous racket, perhaps drawn to the site of the haunting by some preternatural instinct.

The ghost of a murdered boy has been seen running up the bleachers at Del Mar High School's football field. *Photo by Niki Hinds.*

According to the student newspaper from a nearby high school, in 2011, an amateur paranormal investigator conducted an EVP session at the field and recorded an audible response. The investigator asked, "We just want to know why you're here," and a boy's voice replied, "Okay." The voice didn't match any of the investigators who were present, nor had any of them spoken aloud. More recently, the grandmother of a current student swears she heard the sounds of crying coming from the field at night when the school was deserted.

Whose disembodied voice echoes through the night? Is it the ghost of the murdered boy, doomed to relive the last terrifying moments of his life, trying to communicate with the corporeal humans who populate the halls of Del Mar? Or is there a more practical explanation? Perhaps the cries are simply a prank from living, breathing teenagers. School grounds are closed after dark, but apparently someone, living or dead, hasn't gotten the message. Perhaps you will be the one to hear the screams for help or see someone on the bleachers who shouldn't be there—and maybe isn't really there after all.

DOVE HILL ELEMENTARY

Elementary schools should be places of joy for children, places where young minds are broadened and youthful friendships are forged. They shouldn't inspire terror, fear or dread and certainly shouldn't house monstrous apparitions that lurk in the dark. But that's just what lies in wait at one school in the Silver Creek neighborhood.

On the east side of Highway 101 stands Dove Hill Elementary School, which educated local students from 1980 until its closure in 2020. Surrounded by compact single-family homes and adjoining a neighborhood park, the school is, despite its peaceful appearance, the site of a disturbing haunting. Nighttime visitors to the campus report seeing the unexpected figure of a phantom boy, dressed like any other child, wandering near the basketball courts. Those who have gotten close notice that the child has a name tag on his shirt that reads "Michael T." The name tag is bizarre, but there's something else downright terrifying about him: People who get close claim that the boy has no face, just smooth skin where his features should be.

The chilling figure has been seen numerous times throughout the years by students, teachers, parents and other visitors who never expected to

A faceless boy haunts Dove Hill Elementary School. *Author photo.*

encounter such a sad, gruesome specter. According to one report, a teacher was leaving campus late in the evening when she noticed a boy hanging around the basketball courts. She thought it odd that a child would be alone at the school at that time of day, so, thinking he needed assistance, she approached him to ask what he was doing on campus so late. As she got closer to the boy, close enough to read the name tag sticker on his shirt, he turned toward her, and she saw his smooth, blank face—and she ran.

Other visitors, including a group of boys playing late-night basketball, have seen lights inside the empty classrooms turn on and off. Is it the ghost of Michael T., trying to get someone's attention? Or is Dove Hill Elementary haunted by two—or more—spirits? Whatever the answer, this is a haunting that is both terrifying and tragic. If you don't wish to see the faceless apparition for yourself, avoid the otherwise quiet grounds of Dove Hill.

INDEPENDENCE HIGH

Independence High School, just northeast of downtown San Jose, was founded in 1976 and has the largest student population, over three thousand, of any high school in the city. It also has at least one incredibly active theater ghost.

Theaters have a reputation for being hot spots of paranormal activity. Successful productions depend on consistency of both words and actions; with few exceptions, each performance of a play should be identical to the ones that came before. This necessity for repetition lends itself to other behaviors that are part of theater culture. These include rituals, such as leaving a "ghost light" burning in an empty venue to either frighten away or provide lighting for spirits that linger. Superstitions, such as refraining from whistling backstage, are also prevalent. Those who believe in superstitions are often also open to believing in the paranormal, which might explain why actors and stagehands experience ghostly encounters at a higher rate than do those whose minds are not so accepting. Too, dramatic performances rely on the accurate expression of human emotions by actors; they require a great expenditure of energy to communicate these roles convincingly. Ghosts may find that this surplus of energy in the environment acts as a battery of sorts to help them manifest so they can interact with the living. Theater arts educator Jeff Bengford explains further: "We are always creating moments that are beyond the ordinary—no one would pay to see something 'normal' on stage—so we create extraordinary, fantastical moments in the theater. Our audiences come to the theater wanting to believe in the impossible—they come to see and hear a story and we, as Theatre artists, ask them to suspend their disbelief and go with us in a journey as we take them to places beyond the ordinary. So maybe ghosts just feel welcome in the theater." This notion of "beyond the ordinary" aligns precisely with what we call the "paranormal," increasing the likelihood of a spectral encounter in the theatrical realm.

The theater at Independence High School perfectly exemplifies the trope of the haunted theater. Here, it is the ghost of a mysterious man, often heard but rarely seen, that frequently makes its presence known to students and staff. Rumor has it that the man was a janitor who fell to his death from the catwalks above the stage, but Kellye Dodd, longtime dance educator at the school who has experienced unusual events for decades, refutes this claim. However, while she can't say definitively who the spirit is, it was she who gave him the name George in 1990. While not an ominous or threatening spirit, George nevertheless inspires fear and trepidation in those who cross paths with him, especially as he seems more active if one is alone in the theater. Sounds of banging and knocking on the walls often reverberate through the empty space; footsteps can be heard moving along the empty catwalks. Lights flash off and on mysteriously when no one is around to control them, and teachers have caught glimpses of shadows moving past the box office when they are alone in the building. While standing on the stage, teachers and students have seen movement in the control booth at the back of the theater, shadowy figures that disappear when faced directly. Dodd has found items out of place in her office, and another teacher opened the door to the office to feel a cold rush of wind go past her, as though an invisible presence was bursting through the door. According to anecdotes from students over the years, George has definite musical opinions that he's not shy about sharing. He doesn't seem to care for songs by Michael Jackson, pushing the fast-forward button on whatever device is playing songs by the "King of Pop."

Another phenomenon that often reoccurs is that a seat, usually the same one, folds down when it shouldn't, as if an invisible, heavy body is sitting there. During a production of *Macbeth*, Dodd had a hair-raising experience that confirmed her belief there is something unexplainable in the theater. Her co-director had brought his dog to rehearsal, and throughout the night, the dog sat in front of a certain seat, which was folded down although no one was sitting in it. The dog whined and whined, staring intently at the seat

The activity in the theater of Independence High School is attributed to a ghost named George. *Author photo.*

all night. Then, without warning, the seat folded itself up, and the dog stood and trotted away, now completely relaxed.

In 2009, a group of local paranormal investigators spent several hours alone in the building. Throughout the night, they explored the main stage and office areas, attempting to communicate with George and looking for any activity they could document as proof of his existence. Though they were able to disprove some claims to their satisfaction, such as noisy air ducts and sticky springs on some of the seats, they did capture something they couldn't explain. During an EVP session, when the team was recording audio, they captured an unexplained sound, a breathy voice saying, "Matthew." Dodd thinks this was in reference to a student at the time who was involved in theater productions. Perhaps George was calling out a student he was particularly fond of. Despite the group finding no conclusive evidence of a ghost, Dodd remains convinced that something is happening that defies explanation.

The theater at Independence High School proves the theory that acting and the uncanny go hand in hand. Audiences are willing to believe whatever fantasies actors can bring to life, and ghosts—including George—belong in this liminal space between our understanding and our imagination.

Muwekma Ohlone Middle

For many adolescent students, the idea of participating in a physical education class is nothing short of a nightmare. Undressing in front of peers and the potential of being chosen last on a team can be downright distressing. For one unfortunate student at a middle school on the northern edge of Japantown in San Jose, her nightmare continues—even after death. Muwekma Ohlone Middle School was known for nearly eight decades as Burnett Academy. Despite the name change in 2019, the story of the ghost who haunts the girls' locker room persists.

There is a door in the locker room that leads to a classroom upstairs. Long ago, popular belief holds, a student running up the stairs tripped and fell and died as a result of her injuries. Students now claim that when you're in the locker room at night, you can hear pattering noises from the stairwell behind the closed door, like a person moving quickly up and down the stairs. Sometimes there are a series of thumps on the stairway, as if a body has fallen and landed heavily. Many of the reports come from cheerleaders using the locker room after evening basketball games. They also claim to hear the

Muwekma Ohlone Middle School, near San Jose's Japantown. *Author photo.*

disembodied sounds of a female crying from behind the locked door. If the noises the cheerleaders hear are truly the ghost of the dead girl, it seems that, sadly, she is doomed to repeat her last moments on earth. Let this be a lesson to current and future students to tread mindfully. Middle school probably isn't the place you want to be stuck for eternity. Whatever other changes are in the future for this school, it's assured this victim of her own haste will remain part of the lore.

NOTRE DAME HIGH

Notre Dame High School is one of San Jose's oldest educational institutions. The story of the campus ghost has been circulating for many years, but the truth behind that story has been buried almost as long as the legend itself has been around.

In 1851, Notre Dame College was founded on Santa Clara Street in downtown San Jose by a group of Catholic Sisters who came to California from France. Originally serving as both a day school and a boarding school and providing secondary and post-secondary education, the college relocated north to the Peninsula in 1923, while the high school remained on Santa Clara Street. In 1928, the school moved to its present location at Second and Reed. Eminent local judge and philanthropist Honorable Myles P. O'Connor and his wife, Amanda, had gifted their large home to the Sisters in 1898, and this house formed the heart of the new high school campus.

O'Connor was notable for founding the O'Connor Sanitarium on San Carlos Street (which later became O'Connor Hospital, still in operation today two miles west of its original location). Before it housed the high school, the O'Connors' former home was used by the Sisters for an orphanage, called the Notre Dame Institute. After the orphanage moved to Saratoga in 1923, the nuns used the home as a community dwelling and then part of the high school. The O'Connor mansion was irreparably damaged in the 1989 Loma Prieta earthquake and in 2002 was replaced by three-story Manley Hall. The mansion's original fireplace and one glass door are incorporated into the new building, which may explain why ghosts connected with the early decades of the school are said to be felt in the present-day edifice.

The primary legend associated with the campus is all the more tragic because it involves a woman of the sisterhood. Long ago, at an

The O'Connor house was donated to the Sisters of Notre Dame and used as an orphanage. *1890 Myles P. O'Connor residence. Courtesy of San Jose Public Library, California Room, Clyde Arbuckle Photograph Collection.*

undetermined date, a Sister who worked at the school supposedly became pregnant. In what capacity she was employed—teacher or other staff— we don't know, and the story certainly doesn't report who the father was. But it does tell us that, in despair, feeling isolated and knowing she would be excommunicated from the Catholic Church, the pregnant nun hanged herself from a balcony, presumably one that extended from the second floor of the O'Connor mansion.

This story is the best-known myth circulating on campus today, although it is unsubstantiated. There is another death, however, that is confirmed by newspaper accounts from the time. Most people who whisper about the ghosts of nuns at Notre Dame seem to have no idea about this true event. On March 1, 1915, when the O'Connor house was still being used as an orphanage, a nun named Sister Clare was in the basement of the home lighting a heater when there was a sudden, violent gas explosion. The heavy iron door of the heater was flung open, striking her directly in the head. Sister Clare was helped upstairs to her bedroom, where she was treated with all available remedies of the time, but later that night, in the company of another nun, Sister Clare "began to grow weaker. Before any assistance could be summoned, she had breathed her last." An article in the March 3,

Manley Hall includes a fireplace and glass door original to the O'Connor house. *Author photo*.

1915 edition of the *San Jose Mercury Herald* reported that the children under Sister Clare's care were left "almost inconsolable in their grief over the loss of the only mother that many of them ever knew."

Though there are no visual reports of apparitions at the high school, many students report strange feelings on campus, especially on the third floor of Manley Hall, the building that replaced the O'Connor mansion. Students feel as if they're being watched or as if there is a presence around them, even when there is no one else in sight. Those who have experienced these sensations describe them as "spooky." Even some of the staunchest skeptics admit that there might be something unexplained and even supernatural lingering at Notre Dame.

Was there really a pregnant nun who took her own life in the building that once stood here? Or is the invisible presence that of Sister Clare, no longer able to tend to the children placed in her care but watching over the students on campus as if they were her own? If this is the case, this is one haunting that is less frightening than it is comforting—and, at any rate, undeniably sad.

OVERFELT HIGH

Those who work in schools, whether they are teachers, administrators or other staff, are often extremely dedicated to their jobs, willing—and sometimes expected—to go the extra mile for their students. One staff member at Overfelt High School embodies—or perhaps *dis*embodies—this dedication, even from beyond the grave.

Overfelt is located in east San Jose, kitty-corner from Clyde L. Fischer Middle School and behind Reid-Hillview Airport. A janitor was allegedly killed on campus in the 1980s, and he is said to have never left, haunting

A ghostly janitor carries on his life's work at Overfelt High School. *Author photo.*

the school at night and continuing to perform the tasks that were his responsibility in life. Visitors to the school at night report hearing the sound of a janitor's cart, although it is after hours and no employees are working. They hear the wheels rolling and squeaking, the rumbling as the cart passes over the concrete. The sound gets louder and louder and seems as if it's coming closer and closer, but nothing—and no one—ever appears.

Besides the spectral janitor carrying out his duties, the swimming pool is said to be haunted by a student who drowned there. Students speak of a ghost beneath the water who, terrifyingly, claws at them while they swim, perhaps desperate for company, trying to get them to join her in her watery grave. Despite the stories, there are no reported deaths of students or staff on campus, although throughout the school's sixty-year history there have been several violent incidents on or near campus, including most recently the stabbing of a student. With such energy permeating the environment, it does not seem impossible that the spirits of those who walked the campus in life still remain, tethered to the school even in death.

Piedmont Hills High

In the densely populated Berryessa neighborhood at the northern edge of San Jose is Piedmont Hills High School. Its mascot is a pirate, but the campus is rumored to be haunted by ghosts.

The origins of the first story are vague, and the details that have been handed down since the school's inception in 1965 make it impossible to verify the story at all. But legend has it that the parents of a young girl died in a car crash—whether near campus or not is unclear. Somehow, she was left by herself at the school, purportedly to wait in vain for her parents' return. On learning of their deaths, she despaired of her abandonment and, still on school grounds, took her own life. Most agree that she hanged herself. Now, the lonely girl walks the halls of Piedmont Hills, opening and closing doors and following students walking alone, perhaps hoping they're coming to take her home.

That's not the only tragedy associated with the school. In March 2015, a teacher and students preparing for the first PE class of the morning pulled back the swimming pool cover to reveal a body at the bottom of the pool. Though there was early speculation that the death of the twenty-three-year-old man was the result of foul play, it was finally ruled a suicide, and the

The ghost of an orphaned girl walks the halls of Piedmont Hills High School in the Berryessa neighborhood. *Author photo.*

victim appeared to have no connection with the school. However, students and staff were understandably shaken by the discovery. In the following days, rumors began to fly. Students reported seeing shadows on the pool deck and hearing faint splashing with no one in the water. With good reason, even after the pool was cleared to reopen, many were reluctant to set foot in the water.

Sightings of the young man and unexplained activity at the pool seem to have diminished as time goes by, and he may no longer be a presence at the school. But stories of the young girl looking for her parents live on. If you find yourself alone on campus, listen for footsteps behind you and watch for shadows from the corner of your eye. You might see at least one of the lost souls trapped at Piedmont Hills.

SILVER CREEK HIGH

North of the Silver Creek Country Club and east of the Dove Hill neighborhood, where a faceless little boy loiters in the dark, sits Silver Creek High School. The neighborhood was named after a tributary to Coyote

Silver Creek High School boasts a haunted theater. *Author photo.*

Creek, and the school opened its doors in 1969. Like many high schools in the city, especially on the East Side, the school plays host to not only living students but also, possibly, a dead one.

The ghost of a girl named Amy haunts the theater, another spirit drawn to the energy that percolates in such a dramatic, dynamic environment. For reasons unknown and at an undetermined date, she hanged herself in the bathroom right behind the stage. Details of Amy's supernatural activities are few and far between, but her presence is used to explain strange events that occur both inside and outside the theater building. Disembodied voices can be heard faintly echoing through the halls when there seems to be no people on campus. Exterior security lights flicker and sometimes shut off completely. Is it the result of faulty wiring? Or is it a paranormal influence?

Two boys bold enough to investigate the school at night recorded their exploits on video, hoping to catch proof of paranormal activity. While they were standing quietly outside the theater, they claimed to see a door opening by itself and then heard footsteps close to them. These are faintly audible on the video, though no other person appears to be present. Is Amy able to leave the building in which she allegedly met her death? Or is there another entity that roams the campus? There are no confirmed deaths at the school, so perhaps these are merely legends passed down by generations of teenagers. Or perhaps there is someone—or something—that you, too, might spot in the dark at Silver Creek High School.

SLONAKER ELEMENTARY

A number of elementary schools opened in San Jose in 1980, the result of a population boom that saw the number of residents increase by over 200,000. One of these schools was Harry Slonaker Elementary School, located near Overfelt High School and its ghostly janitor, just east of Highway 101. In 2013, the school closed because of declining enrollment, and the campus is now used as a charter middle school. But during its initial tenure as a public school, Slonaker Elementary managed to gain a haunted reputation.

The primary claims of alarmed staff and visitors were the sounds of children playing outside. This may not seem odd at an elementary school, but the noise occurred either while all students were in class or after school hours, when no students were on campus. Some people said they heard children screaming, but it's unclear whether these were shouts of joy stemming from children's play or cries of distress. Either way, this type of activity seems to be residual, an imprint of the normal cacophony associated with a place where children gather, repeating itself without consciousness or intelligence.

One persistent rumor that may or may not be related to the sounds heard on campus concerns a child who was hit and killed by a car driven by his uncle, presumably while the boy was being picked up from or dropped off at school. There is no documentation of any deaths at the school, although it's entirely possible that a traffic fatality involving a child occurred nearby at some point during the school's operation.

An interesting side note is that the school was named after Harry E. Slonaker, a community leader who was active in his hometown of Chicago in the Boys Brotherhood Republic (BBR), an organization designed to teach boys responsibility through civic and recreational activities. In 1944, Slonaker settled in San Jose and founded Boys City, which he modelled on BBR. He served as its director until 1971, when he retired. Throughout his adult life, he dedicated himself to the prevention of juvenile delinquency and advocated for underserved youth. Perhaps Slonaker would be gratified to know that the playful sounds that echo through his namesake school are those of the children he worked tirelessly to champion and protect.

3
SAN JOSE STATE UNIVERSITY

S an Jose State University, known familiarly as San Jose State or SJSU, is San Jose's institution of higher learning in the heart of downtown. Founded in 1857 as the first California State Normal School, it was the first institution of public higher education in the West and originally a college for training teachers, mostly young women. Interestingly, the San Jose campus opened a branch in 1882 in Los Angeles that would become UCLA. In 1934, San Jose's normal school was folded into the state college system and earned university status in 1972. Now, it covers 154 acres, with boundaries extending from Fourth to Eleventh Streets and from San Fernando to San Salvador Streets and adjunct facilities such as Spartan Stadium nearby. It's known primarily as a commuter school, serving students from around the area; over 80 percent of its nearly thirty-six thousand students live off campus. Business and engineering are the most popular majors, and a campus extracurricular activity might as well be ghost hunting, as stories about phantoms at the college have existed for decades.

HOOVER HALL

The building most likely to be talked about in hushed voices around a campfire—or during freshman orientation—is Hoover Hall, one of six three-story brick dormitories on the southeast side of campus. This group

Tower Hall, built in 1910, and Morris Dailey Auditorium are among the oldest structures on San Jose State University's campus. *Author photo.*

of six, which opened in 1960, was known collectively as "The Bricks" and is still called that today, although five of the buildings have been removed. One of the demolished buildings, Hoover Hall, was the epicenter of a number of paranormal claims, including showers turning on in the women's bathroom on the first floor and reports of menacing and uncomfortable feelings in the first-floor rooms. Many residents said they never felt completely alone in their rooms, even when no one else was with them. The building, in its most notorious ghost story, also hosted a haunted phone booth and the spirit of a murder victim who replayed the last moments of her life in a graphic residual haunting. Legend has it that a young woman was attacked in a hallway somewhere on the second floor on the way to her room. Terrified and bleeding from her injuries, she ran screaming down the stairs with her knife-wielding attacker in pursuit. She attempted to find safety in the telephone booth in the lobby of the building, even getting as far as dialing the first two digits of 911, when her attacker caught up with her and dispatched her with several vicious stabs of his knife. She bled to death in the phone booth, her lifeblood staining the walls and floor around her. Generations of

Washburn Hall is the last remaining dormitory of the classic six known as "The Bricks." *Author photo.*

students in the building spread stories of her bloody figure running down the stairs, screaming for help; those attempting to use the telephone in the booth often found it out of order, as it would only dial the numbers 9 and 1. Later, as cell phones became ubiquitous and telephone booths obsolete, the booth was removed from the building. But some students claimed to hear the phone ringing in the middle of the night, even though it was no longer there. Perhaps it was the young woman calling for help from beyond the grave.

School historians maintain that the first murder on campus didn't occur until well after this story was established, but that didn't stop it from gaining mythological traction. Students and paranormal investigators hoping to catch sight of the fleeing ghost will be disappointed, however, as Hoover Hall was razed in 2016 to make way for the Campus Village buildings. The only remaining dormitory of the classic six, Washburn Hall, has now inherited the moniker "The Bricks." One wonders if the screaming ghost of the bloody girl has likewise migrated to haunt this space, or maybe she appears inside the new buildings that rise in the stead of Hoover Hall. Only time will tell if she'll make another appearance.

JOE WEST HALL

Joe West Hall is another residence building, between Washburn and Campus Village. Built in 1968, it's also referred to as a "Classic" (and sometimes the "Waffle Tower" for its protruding window frames). The twelve-story building houses 650 students and is named after a former dean and registrar at SJSU. The building has a troubled history, weighed down by the pall cast by a number of deaths and other ordeals.

In a 2013 article in the campus newspaper *Spartan Daily*, history lecturer Eric Narveson refers to a death in the late 1960s that occurred either in or near the dorm building, when a radical protester built a homemade bomb, "probably trying to take out Joe West Hall. Narveson said that instead, the man prematurely detonated the bomb and killed himself." However, a university spokesperson said in 1995 that "the last residence hall student suicide was in 1968, but *did not occur on campus*" (emphasis added). This was reported in the *Spartan Daily* on September 25, 1995, when a student fell to his death from an upper window of Joe West. It's unclear whether the bomb

Joe West Hall, the site of a number of deaths. *Author photo*.

story is apocryphal, but it adds to the legend surrounding the dormitory and, if true, presents a possible character who could still remain in the building.

Another confirmed suicide occurred in 2014, and a student passed away in her room from unidentified causes in 2003. In 2001, an arson fire destroyed benches and fences on the concrete walkway between the dorm and the dining commons building behind it. The arsonist was never apprehended, and many residents were left shaken and fearful for their safety in the aftermath of the fire.

Claims of activity at Joe West Hall are standard haunted-house fare: doors opening and closing on their own without even a breeze to shift them; voices echoing from empty hallways and stairwells; a fleeting but oppressive atmosphere that greets residents and visitors as they walk on certain floors, as though the air is thick and heavy. Without full-body apparitions or direct communication from the other side, it's difficult to ascertain which spirit or spirits might be responsible for the paranormal phenomena. But it seems safe to surmise that the tragic manner in which some students met their deaths and lingering negative energy from the fire and other traumatic events that happened inside the walls could provide the fuel that spirits need to manifest or could act as a battery for residual hauntings. As long as new residents continue to bring their energy and life forces into the building, whatever remains at Joe West Hall will have the power it needs to make its presence known.

YOSHIHIRO UCHIDA HALL

Uchida Hall, on the corner of Fourth Street and Paseo de San Antonio, is part of the massive Spartan Gym complex, which in its entirety houses a gymnasium, locker rooms, team lounges and offices and training and weight rooms for various sports. In its original incarnation, before it was renamed for a beloved and influential judo coach, the building contained—and was known simply as—the men's gymnasium. It is this portion of the complex that retains the haunting memories of a terrible chapter in American history.

In 1942, the men's gym was used as a registration and collection point, euphemistically called a "Civil Control Station," for Japanese Americans being sent to internment camps. Two months after America's entrance into World War II, President Franklin Roosevelt signed Executive Order 9066, which forced Americans of Japanese descent—including those who had as little as one-sixteenth Japanese ancestry—to pack what belongings they could carry and relocate to internment camps far from the Pacific coast. After registering at San Jose State, Japanese Americans, of whom four thousand lived in Santa Clara County and two-thirds of whom were American citizens, were sent by train to assembly centers, many in Southern California, where they were formally processed and then incarcerated in prisons scattered across the western United States, such as Manzanar and Tule Lake in California and Topaz in Utah.

Many people in San Jose and throughout the United States experienced the internment for themselves. But for the rest of the population, it's difficult to comprehend the fear and anxiety surrounding that traumatic experience. Imagine receiving notification on May 23, 1942, that you, as an enemy of the state, must turn yourself in. You arrive the next day for registration at the men's gym at San Jose State College. You are given an identification number, stripping you of your individual identity, and are instructed to report in one week to a train station. Now you know without a doubt that you are going away, with no certainty of returning. After finishing registration at the gymnasium, you and your family pack what belongings you can carry and, if you are lucky, make arrangements with sympathetic friends and neighbors to care for your pets and your property in your absence. If you are unlucky, you sell what items you can before you leave, lock your doors and hope for the best, knowing that once you are gone your home and land will be sold cheaply. You will never receive the profits or be able to recover what has essentially been stolen from you. You will have no home to come back to, if you ever do come home.

You make your own way to the railroad station at the appointed time and day, boarding a train against your will, trying to keep your family close and your children calm. The train ride ends at a holding area, such as in Pomona, California. After a few months there, you are shipped to a detention center in a desert or another godforsaken place where you are imprisoned for the next three and a half years, until the end of the war.

This was the reality. We don't need ghosts to make it a terrifying, haunting story.

The family of Yoshihiro Uchida, for whom the men's gym was renamed in 1997, experienced this horror for themselves. Uchida studied chemical engineering at San Jose State and in 1940 was appointed student coach of the judo program. When the war began, he was drafted to serve as a laboratory technician for the U.S. Army while his family was processed through the registration center at the men's gymnasium. His parents were sent to a

Yoshihiro Uchida Hall, now part of the Spartan Gym complex, was a registration center for Japanese American internees in 1942. *Author photo.*

camp in Arizona. His brothers went to Tule Lake, and his sister and her husband were incarcerated in Idaho. At the end of the war, Uchida returned to San Jose State and completed a degree in biology, continuing to coach judo part-time while working at a hospital laboratory. His commitment to judo, including establishing it as a collegiate sport, led to him coaching the first U.S. Olympic judo team in 1964 and earning a bronze medal. He later became a successful businessman and civic leader, developing housing and businesses in San Jose's Japantown.

Despite his athletic success, Uchida continued to face racism and discrimination as a Japanese American, the echoes of which still haunt the SJSU campus today. For years, students, staff and visitors to campus have heard the sounds of crying and faint human voices coming from inside the old gymnasium, and these are attributed to the Japanese people who were forced to report here in 1942. It's important to remember that this building was a registration center, not a detention center, and people would not have been held here for extended periods of time. No deaths were reported in the building or during the registration process. But as we've seen in other instances, loss of life is not a prerequisite for a haunting. Stress, anxiety and trauma can pollute a location or environment and lead to negative spiritual manifestations. The imminent incarceration of the Japanese population was an agonizing experience. The whole matter was frightening and shocking on its own, and perhaps the stories that are told about disembodied voices and supernatural weeping serve as important reminders of the real horrors of history. We must use these ghosts of the past to make sure this kind of tragedy never happens again.

4

HOTELS

SAINTE CLAIRE HOTEL

The Westin San Jose looks like it should be haunted, and it doesn't disappoint. Built in 1926, the Sainte Claire Hotel, as it was formerly (and is still colloquially) known, on the southeast corner of Market and San Carlos Streets, was nicknamed the "million-dollar hotel" for the cost of building and furnishing it—a goodly sum in those days. It was the largest and most elegant hotel between San Francisco and Los Angeles and is now listed in the National Register of Historic Places. Though it fell into disrepute in the 1970s and stood empty for a time in the late 1980s, preservationists were eventually successful in saving the landmark edifice, returning it to its former grandeur in 1992. Now operated by a prominent hotel chain, the Westin continues to be a luxury destination in the heart of downtown San Jose. It also continues to make perennial lists of the nation's most haunted hotels.

The most active ghost at the Sainte Claire can be traced to a familiar haunted trope: that of a jilted bride. Legend has it that in the 1930s, a woman named Julia was eagerly anticipating her wedding. With her family and guests gathered in the Palm Room and a lavish reception awaiting the happy couple, Julia walked down the aisle to the altar and waited for her groom. And waited…and waited. He never showed, having run off with another woman.

Construction of the Sainte Claire Hotel in 1926. *Sainte Claire Hotel. Courtesy of San Jose Public Library, California Room, Clyde Arbuckle Photograph Collection.*

Devastated and humiliated, her guests calling after her to no avail, Julia ran in despair to the basement of the hotel, where she hanged herself from an overhead pipe. (Some stories report that she ran to the roof and threw herself off the top.)

Today, the sounds of high heels clicking rapidly across the floor can be heard throughout the hotel. The footsteps are sharp and angry-sounding, as though their invisible owner is in a state of emotional agitation, perhaps patrolling the halls looking for acts of infidelity in the guest rooms. The strangest thing about these tapping heels? The floors are carpeted.

Employees of the hotel also experience Julia's presence as a disagreeable feeling in the offices and find paperwork disturbed and rearranged. A guest of the hotel who was taking pictures near the Palm Room claimed to capture the disembodied feet and legs of what looked like a bride.

Other sightings include a boy around ten years old spotted sitting on various stairways; men and women entering the lounge elegantly dressed in styles from the early twentieth century; and clearly audible noises from rooms that are not occupied.

There are also stories about what is referred to as the "smoking ghost" and a poltergeist. These could be residual phenomena from previous incarnations of the property. From 1851 until it was torn down in 1920, the Eagle Brewery, the first beer brewery in Santa Clara County, occupied the corner of Market and San Carlos. Surely, there were workplace accidents resulting in deaths; perhaps some of the more rough-around-the-edges spirits reported in the hotel can be attributed to this period in the site's history. Or maybe the ghosts result from the era when the Sainte Claire (and the majority of downtown San Jose) sank into disrepair, when the hotel was used to shelter transients. Author Jeff Dwyer, in his book *Ghost Hunters' Guide to the San Francisco Bay Area*, claims that victims of substance abuse died inside the building. Maybe their last resting place became their eternal stomping grounds.

Much of the activity seems to center on the second and sixth floors, although some sources reference the third floor as a hot spot, and there are reports that span the entirety of the hotel, including the lobby. Many employees are afraid to enter certain areas alone; others won't even talk about a potential haunting at the hotel, whether due to fear or disbelief. Perhaps those disbelievers will be convinced when they finally have a run-in with the spirits of the Sainte Claire that checked in but will never check out.

THE FAIRMONT

Most San Jose residents are familiar with our Japantown, a neighborhood north of City Hall that's one of the last few authentic Japantowns in the country. But San Jose was also once home to a thriving Chinatown, which experienced several tragedies that may be responsible for some of the ghosts that haunt downtown's Fairmont Hotel. The Fairmont opened in 1987 and was immediately presented as the crown jewel of San Jose's revitalized downtown. Located on Market Street directly east of the Plaza de Cesar Chavez, its centralized location and proximity to attractions such as the Tech Interactive, San Jose Museum of Art, Cathedral Basilica of San Jose and the San Jose McEnery Convention Center places it at the nucleus of the city. The hotel has gone through some financial crises and, at the time of this writing, has been purchased by the Hilton brand, but most residents still know it as the Fairmont. Both the hotel and the surrounding environs are

The front entrance of the Fairmont Hotel on Market Street. *Author photo.*

said to be haunted. To discover the origins of the spirits, it's necessary to take a somewhat winding tour through the history of the city's founding.

The Fairmont may not be the city's most historic hotel, but it sits on one of the oldest portions of downtown (though not of the city proper). In 1797, after suffering repeated flooding of the Guadalupe River, the pueblo of San Jose moved about a mile and a half south from its original location on what is now Hobson Street just west of First Street. (The historical marker commemorating the spot is actually located at 151 West Mission Street, the former site of City Hall.) Relocation of the pueblo, or civilian town, which involved reestablishing the center of town and government, led the settlers to the present-day Plaza de Cesar Chavez, on Market and San Fernando Streets. Much of the new settlement consisted of adobe dwellings for the settlers and their families, such as the Peralta Adobe, which has been preserved adjacent to the San Pedro Market. The *juzgado*, or town hall, was constructed in 1798 at what is now Post and Market Streets. The building that stands there today inspires whispers of ghosts. This is not surprising, considering the history of the land. In addition to its use as the center of city government, the juzgado served as courthouse and jail, certainly accommodating at some point those with violent or criminal tendencies who may have left a negative energetic imprint on the area. In 1846, in an emotionally charged event during the Mexican-American War, the American flag was raised for the first time in Santa Clara County, over the juzgado building. In 1902, the Alcantara Building, still standing today, was constructed on that corner. It housed the Metropole Hotel, a working-class inn for new arrivals to the valley. At some point by 1915, a saloon that was featured in the Charlie Chaplin film *A Night Out* was operating in the building.

The proprietor of the saloon, Chick Leddy, was also a bootlegger and racketeer who had his business license revoked after selling whiskey illegally. In 1928, he was convicted of murdering a salesman in another saloon he operated nearby, striking the man with a mattock. It's highly probable that Leddy's temper followed him from bar to bar, making it unlikely that his 1928 murder was his first. Could the eerie, unsettled sensation many report outside of the Alcantara Building actually stem from an unknown victim of Leddy's rage? Or are the shadows that dart around corners, sometimes seen by those peering through the front windows of the empty building, related to the poor souls who lived here during its incarnation as a transient hostel in the 1980s? Perhaps they can be attributed to the same tormented souls who are also believed to haunt the Fairmont, dating to one of the ugliest times in San Jose's history.

Prior to construction of the Fairmont, one mere block from the history-laden site of the juzgado, archaeological excavations in the area of Market and San Fernando revealed a treasure trove of artifacts dating to San Jose's first Chinatown, located in this area beginning in 1866. Over one thousand people lived in this area, which consisted of apartment buildings, businesses, restaurants, a temple and a theater. Chinese residents were proactive and protective members of their community, organizing a civilian fire brigade and filling nearby water tanks to access in case of fire. However, on May 4, 1887, a massive blaze spread suddenly and rapidly through Chinatown while most residents were away from their homes. The fire, later determined to be arson, was checked by the phenomenal efforts of the Chinese fire brigade and a city fire company. These efforts allowed nearby non-Chinese structures to remain unharmed. But since the Chinese water tanks had been drained in an act of sabotage, Chinatown was completely decimated.

After the fire, city leaders razed and flattened the rubble, burying the evidence that a Chinese settlement had ever existed in the area. The community moved elsewhere, eventually settling near Sixth Street adjacent to Japantown. During excavation for the Fairmont in the mid-1980s, remnants of the long-past Chinese settlers once again saw the light of day, as the ephemera of their daily lives, as well as items that must have been especially cherished, were unearthed. The archive, which includes ceramics, cooking and dining implements, medicines and cosmetics, paintbrushes, ebony dominoes and dolls, can be viewed today at the Chinese American Historical Museum at History San José in Kelley Park. Perhaps visitors will hear whispers of once-silenced voices speaking through these items.

A historical marker on the corner of the Fairmont building commemorates the fire, and some believe that the spectral energy of the tragedy has crept into the building itself. While no lives were lost in the fire, it's entirely possible that the trauma and violence of the era could have created a residual haunting that plays out in the hotel today. Many employees and visitors report odd activity, such as doors that open and close by themselves and lights that turn on and off with no explanation. Guests on multiple floors have been awakened by loud voices coming from the room next door, only to call the front desk and be informed that there are no occupants in the neighboring room. The suicide of a guest a few years ago may have added to the specters haunting the halls. The incident involved poisonous chemicals that spread throughout several floors, sending guests in nearby rooms to the hospital.

The hotel will remain empty as it undergoes the transition to new ownership, leaving whatever ghosts are inside to roam the rooms unseen. But as we know from the layers of history throughout that portion of downtown, the ghosts of the Fairmont aren't the only spirits with claims to the land. Visit the plaza along Market Street, and it's guaranteed you'll be surrounded by the past—and probably some ghosts.

Le Baron Hotel / Holiday Inn Silicon Valley

In the 1970s, before redevelopment, downtown San Jose was not for the faint of heart. In fact, for most residents and families in the surrounding areas, downtown was a grimy, crime-infested ghost town to be avoided. Jobs, retail and City Hall moved away from the city center. An expanded highway and expressway system made it easier to bypass downtown altogether. The Fairmont had yet to be built; hotels that had once been the grandes dames of the city, such as the Sainte Claire, had fallen into disrepair. If they were even still standing, they were being used to house transients. So, when the Le Baron Hotel opened in 1974 at 1350 North First Street in an area that was exploding with new development, it was considered the most modern, luxurious and desirable place to stay in town. Though the hotel has changed hands several times since that grand opening and now operates as a Holiday Inn, it has never lost its haunted reputation. And unlike other locations, where the ghosts originate from the land, the hauntings in this hotel are tied to the building itself.

In his book *Ghost Hunter's Guide to the Bay Area*, Jeff Dwyer tells the story of a traveling salesman who checked into room 538 of the Le Baron. The staff at the front desk reported that he seemed tired and haggard, even despondent, as he received his room key and headed to the fifth floor. The next morning, when the occupant missed the checkout time and concerned staff opened his door, they found his lifeless body on the bed, dead from an apparent overdose of pills. After his death, housekeeping staff who entered the room were shocked and understandably terrified when they encountered his ghost, manifesting as a full-body apparition wearing the dark suit he died in. Subsequent guests who stayed overnight in room 538 reported malfunctioning lights, a radio that turned on unexpectedly and unidentifiable noises. There were also reports of his apparition wandering through the dining room and the hallways of the fourth, fifth and sixth floors, apparently doomed to remain in the hotel where he ended his life.

However, an article in the February 3, 1982 edition of the *San Jose Mercury News* attributes a different origin to the activity in room 538. In 1979, a young woman was found dead in the room of a drug overdose. When housekeeper Lupe Moncivais entered the room several months after the body was found, she claimed to experience the ghost of the young woman for the first time: "I heard a voice from far, far away calling 'Lupe,'" she said in an interview for the article. "Then I heard it again, and I thought someone was trying to play a joke on me. I realized it wasn't a joke when I heard someone whisper my name in my ear like they wanted to ask me something." Shortly after, she felt invisible fingers tugging at her hair, even though she was completely alone.

Around that same time, guests who stayed in the room reported doors slamming, water faucets mysteriously turning on and off and the elevator stopping by itself at the fifth floor. Another housekeeper even witnessed a shimmering woman in white entering the room when it was known to be unoccupied. Jeff Dwyer claims that the suicidal woman was a jilted bride, but this remains unverified. Perhaps the ghost was attempting to communicate her story to Lupe and other staff, but her identity remains a mystery.

In a posting on the Ghostly World website, a user named Tom, who claimed to work for the maintenance department of the hotel in the early

1980s, weighed in with his own experience. After hearing an unexplained scream, Tom ran into another employee, who hinted that he was the source of the mysterious activity: "He told me the story about the hotel supposedly being haunted, so every once in a while he would do something to keep the rumors going because it was good for business. I worked there almost a year and that was the only time I ever heard anything about it."

True-life haunting or publicity stunt perpetrated by members of the staff? Suicidal salesman or betrayed bride-to-be? After a flurry of reported activity in the 1980s, the haunting seems to have diminished considerably. The hotel underwent extensive renovations in 1996 and 2015, when it changed ownership. While construction and remodeling of buildings sometimes stirs up paranormal activity, in this case it seems to have laid it to rest. We may never know the true identity of the ghost that haunts room 538, but it has made an indelible mark on the city's haunted history.

5

RESTAURANTS AND NIGHTLIFE

65 POST STREET / SPLASH VIDEO DANCE BAR

Saloons, bars and clubs are known for their spirits—and the older the building, the more likely it is that the spirits inside are not just the alcoholic kind. The dance club that currently occupies an infamous old building in downtown San Jose is home to more than just cheap drink specials. It also houses some unsavory history—and some serious ghosts.

Unofficially within the bounds of what is considered San Jose's Downtown Historic District, 65 Post Street definitely deserves historic status. The two-story, Italian ornate building on the corner of Post Street and Lightston Alley is likely the oldest commercial structure still standing in San Jose. One of the best-preserved examples of Italianate architecture in San Jose, the current home of Splash Video Dance Bar features myriad decorative details on the second-floor façade such as ornamental hoods over the windows, raised plaster panels and bracketed cornices under the roofline. This elaborate, even showy building was perfectly suited for the shady, debauched activity that was once central to downtown San Jose.

Post Street, now running one block south of Santa Clara Street between Almaden Boulevard and First Street, was once known as El Dorado Street. Originally, in 1855, it was just one short block between First and Market Streets. It was also the heart of San Jose's red-light district. The San Jose Underbelly website describes the scene in appropriately colorful terms:

Splash Video Dance Bar now occupies the historic building at 65 Post Street. *Author photo.*

"One could drink, snort, smoke, and spit amongst like-minded folk. Red lights glittered from second-story windows. Gold moon-light revealed saloons a'plenty. Harlots in peacock attire promised love—for a price." Historian Pat Loomis writes that the block got grittier and seedier with each passing year until it was best known for "painted ladies, lotteries—and for more saloons than any other street in town."

In 1902, the street was renamed in an effort to clean up its image, hoping the ne'er-do-wells who populated the area would be likewise inclined to clean up their act or find a new place to pursue their vices. But it would take more than a change of name to wash clean the reputation of 65 Post Street.

The building started life in 1873 and was from the very beginning used as a saloon and bawdy house, or a brothel (alternately referred to euphemistically as a "boardinghouse"). For the first forty or so years of its life, it was christened, variously, the Orpheus Saloon, the Bird Saloon (allegedly from the live canaries in the windows) and Eugene Votzenlogel's Saloon and Bath House. The last name of one of the building's more colorful owners, Billy Fenerin, was added to its official billing as the Glein-Fenerin Building. Also called Billy Finley because it was easier to pronounce, he purchased the building in 1916 and ran a saloon and gambling hall on the first floor and lived on the second, also working at various times as a bail bondsman, a moneylender and a manager of professional fighters. During Prohibition, Billy kept his business afloat by turning the storefront into a barbershop and selling bootlegged alcohol out the back—a true speakeasy. His establishment was so rough that he eventually lost his bar license due to excessive fighting on the property. While he didn't die on Post Street, he did meet his end by falling from the fourth-story window of a building in San Francisco during the 1956 St. Patrick's Day Parade, a tragic—yet somehow fitting—demise for a man who was the life of the party.

The building remained in the Fenerin family until 1991, cycling through different businesses until it opened in 2011 as Splash Video Dance Bar. The one constant among all the changes throughout the years has been the reports of ghosts. This building is haunted.

It's unclear who remains after the last patrons have gone home and the employees have closed up for the night, but consistent activity has been reported for years. A local paranormal group investigated the club after hours one night. In the course of their investigation, the team seemed to capture evidence of intelligent interaction with the use of dowsing rods, receiving a series of compelling responses to yes-or-no questions. Dowsing rods, a pair of short, L-shaped metal rods traditionally used to find underground water sources, are sometimes used by paranormal investigators to communicate with spirits. During this investigation, the rods appeared to be manipulated by an unseen entity. On the same evening, one investigator saw an arm waving at her from across the room out of the darkness, and another felt as if he was being overcome by an angry, aggressive energy. With the kind of hostile, combative clientele known to frequent the building in its rough-and-tumble days, it's no surprise that some of that bellicose energy might remain, looking for a live human vessel to inhabit.

Greg, a manager at Splash, adds reports of activity he's experienced, maintaining that the resident ghosts are responsible for "glasses flying off the shelf, stuff being moved, hidden from you." Though destructive, the mood of this activity feels more attention-seeking or mischievous than angry, lending credence to the theory that there may be more than one spirit here. Perhaps it is a former lady of the night, desperate not to be forgotten, or one of the former owners who doesn't approve of the way the current business is run.

A brothel, a speakeasy and now a dance club at the center of San Jose's LGBTQ community. With so much life throughout its history and so much energy from the living continuing to permeate its walls, it's no wonder that ghosts don't want to leave this space.

TRIALS PUB

A much-beloved pub in downtown San Jose is often described as a "home away from home" by its regulars. Frequented by neighborhood residents, students of nearby San Jose State University and visitors from all over, Trials Pub claims to be about as authentic a British pub as one can find outside of England. Its historic building, with a long and varied history, also provides a home for active—and dark—spirits.

The building at 265 North First Street, north of St. James Park, is designated as City Landmark no. 77, bestowed in 1992. The two-story structure, built in the Romanesque Revival style, is trimmed with rusticated sandstone, and it features (charmingly, to those who happen to look up) a distinctive ornamental façade on the second floor. Half-round pediments top the center windows, which are bookended by a pair of oriel windows. Gold letters—some missing—above the front door proclaim the building as "The Thomas Victoria," but when it was built it was known at the Tognazzi Building. According to the Preservation Action Council of San Jose, a nonprofit organization with a mission to preserve the city's architectural history, Baptista G. Tognazzi was a Swiss-born grocer who commissioned the edifice in 1892 from William Van Siclen, a prominent local architect who designed numerous buildings nearby. (Tognazzi's name is spelled differently in other sources.) Connected to the Beatrice Building next door, the Tognazzi Building housed a grocery store on the first floor, and the family lived on the second floor. The history is a bit murky, as there are varying claims as to the actual use of the building through the years, but according to city directories, the building was home to a butcher shop in the 1920s and the Penny-a-Dish Cafeteria (a familiar and necessary establishment during the

265 North First Street, the home of Trials Pub, is a city landmark. *Author photo*.

Great Depression) in 1934. By the end of that decade, it was an antiques shop. According to Trials' website, the building was used for a time as a hotel for railroad workers and later as a brothel; that claim is unsubstantiated, though many downtown buildings likely offered this service. The website states that in the 1970s, the United Farm Workers housed its offices in the Thomas Victoria; the first pub at the location opened in 1997.

One of the more popular ghost stories dates to the time when it's said the building was used as an auxiliary jail, housing overflow prisoners from the county jail, which was located within the superior court building a few blocks away and detained those awaiting trial at the courthouse. The most violent prisoners were taken to the basement and held in dark, dank solitary cells, as befitting their atrocious crimes. To this day, remnants of these subterranean cells, now crumbling from decay and neglect, can still be found underneath the pub's dart lane. There are stories of guards savagely mistreating prisoners once they were below ground and out of sight and earshot of those on the upper floors, who expected more proper behavior. One of these prisoners, in a possible act of retaliation, may have killed a relentless guard; or a prisoner driven to the depths of despair by his seemingly hopeless situation may have taken his own life. Either way, one of these miserable souls remains as an intimidating entity that continues to haunt the bowels of the pub. A hulking shadow figure has been seen moving in and out of the decrepit jail cells, disappearing whenever anyone gets too close. Employees and patrons throughout the years have heard scraping and banging sounds when no one is in the basement, and some report an upsetting feeling, bordering on panic, as they attempt to descend to the gloomy cellar. Some employees refuse to go down by themselves, and a few never make it down the stairs at all.

For those patrons unwilling or unable to visit the depths of the popular pub, another reported ghost might be more accessible—at least to those who find they have business to attend to in the women's restroom, which is haunted by another residual resident. There's no word on the origin of this lavatory phantom, and there are not many reports of how she—or he—manifests. But after a few drinks at the pub, you might find yourself in the vicinity of this ghost. Or you might at least work up enough courage to descend the stairs to the basement.

GRANDVIEW RESTAURANT

An elevated cuisine, refined atmosphere, killer valley views and a historic setting: Grandview Restaurant on Mount Hamilton Road has it all for the discerning diner. It even includes a little something for the ghost hunter.

The Grandview began life in 1884 as a tavern, hotel and stagecoach stop for workers building the observatory at the summit of Mount Hamilton and, later, for sightseers journeying up the mountain. In 1875, California's richest man, the eccentric James Lick, who made his fortune in part by building pianos in South America, commissioned the creation of an astronomical observatory as his lasting memorial. After discarding the notions of a giant pyramid in San Francisco and statues of himself and his parents that could be seen from out at sea, he decided, more sensibly, on an observatory. He selected as its site Mount Hamilton, some twenty miles due east of downtown San Jose. He told the Santa Clara County Board of Supervisors that it would be his permanent gift to the state if the county would build the road up to it. Sadly, Lick never got to see his monument in the flesh, as he died in 1876. Lick Observatory was completed in 1888. Operated by the University of California since its inception, it boasts the third-largest refracting telescope in the world and has been instrumental in the discovery of, among other things, twenty-five comets and a new moon of Jupiter. Incidentally, Lick is buried under the telescope and may be the only person in the world to have that distinction.

At its completion, Mount Hamilton Road offered easier access to the summit than the previously used San Felipe Road. After the road was finished, Alanson Story, a successful agriculturist who already owned significant property in San Jose, purchased 1,500 acres of land on the western slope of the mountain. Seeing a prime source of revenue, he built the Grandview House as a convenient—and presumably lucrative—stopping point appreciated by thirsty and weary passengers riding in stagecoaches to visit the observatory. One can assume that the thirsty and weary horses pulling these coaches appreciated the stop as well.

The roadhouse suffered various fires, as wood structures often do, burning down first in 1942 and then again in 1954 after being rebuilt on its original site. The building that houses the restaurant today and delights so many diners with its breathtaking view of the valley below was built in 1956. Believers say it's home to the spirit of a young girl.

The identity of the girl, who witnesses say appears to be nine or ten years old, is shrouded in mystery. Wild and implausible rumors circulate about her origins and the cause of her untimely death. But most people who have experienced her are in agreement about her behavior. She appears throughout the restaurant but primarily on the balcony, gazing out at the view. If anyone approaches, she vanishes immediately, making it difficult for witnesses to describe her with any detail or consistency. She is known to toy with the lights in the dining room, turning them off and on unexpectedly. Other paranormal reports include feeling sudden cold spots in the air, even when the rest of the room maintains its temperature, and hearing the faint sound of voices emanating from empty rooms after hours.

One possible source for this young ghost is undocumented and highly speculative but spine-chilling nevertheless. A legend holds that in the 1950s, in the foothills climbing up to the summit, children began disappearing. It started when one mother, whose family lived in a rural home on one of the hidden lanes that run through the foothills like spiderwebs, called her young daughter to come in from playing outside. There was no response. The woman called a second time, and a third, and eventually the family went looking for her. But she was never seen again.

If the legend is to be believed, this was the first of many disappearances in the vicinity of the Grandview. No one knows the exact number of children who are supposed to have vanished in that decade, but it led to frightened

The balcony of the Grandview Restaurant, where the ghost of a young girl is seen. *Author photo.*

conjecture about a serial kidnapper and killer preying on the children of the mountain. Some even whispered about satanic, possibly cannibalistic cults prowling the hills, like those said to live in other remote areas of San Jose. There's no evidence of missing children during this or any other period in the area's history; this uncorroborated story is almost certainly just an exceptionally disturbing urban legend. But there does seem to be activity at the Grandview Restaurant on Mount Hamilton Road. Take a drive up to the restaurant one summer night and relax on the balcony overlooking the valley. You may be the one to finally uncover the truth about the young ghostly girl.

JOSE THEATRE / SAN JOSE IMPROV

Ghosts are no laughing matter at one comedy club in downtown San Jose. The city's oldest theater, once known as the Jose Theatre, is now home to the San Jose Improv and a haunting attributed to a rumored inferno.

Located at 62 South Second Street, the Jose Theatre was built in 1903 and opened a year later, hosting stock theater companies and vaudeville performances. The man who commissioned and first owned the theater was David Jacks, a landowner and developer from Monterey who was also the namesake of Monterey Jack cheese. At the theater's inception, visiting performers stayed in top-floor apartments. Through at least the 1980s, the kitchens and dorm-like bedrooms were still extant. Popular legend maintains that Harry Houdini and Charlie Chaplin performed at the theater, although this is likely untrue.

Throughout the years, as the building changed hands, it transitioned from hosting vaudeville to silent films to second-run movies and creature features, the latter of which are still fondly remembered by a portion of San Joseans today. After the 1989 Loma Prieta earthquake, the building's owners, prolific local developers, deemed it economically unfeasible to retrofit it. For a time, it seemed that the theater had hosted its final audience. Fortunately, in 1990, the Jose was declared a city landmark and, after being purchased by the City of San Jose, was leased to the Improv comedy club. Famous comedians, including late-night television hosts and *Saturday Night Live* alumni, have performed in this building. But its most compelling performance might be what happens in the theater after dark.

Comedian and San Jose native Anjelah Johnson interviewed David Williams, manager of San Jose Improv, on the February 2021 episode of her podcast *Ghost Stories with Anjelah*. Williams prefaces his comments by saying, "From the very beginning, I was not a believer in this type of thing, but I've definitely become converted." He claims that the green room, where performers wait and socialize before and after their sets, has a "very mischievous," not malicious, energy. One of his experiences illustrates this. One warm summer evening, Williams opened all the windows of the green room. He stepped out of the room for a moment and noted that the windows were still open on his return. After just a few minutes of being alone in the room, he looked again and saw that the windows he had opened were closed.

Performers and staff also feel a darker energy in the dressing room underneath the stage, where in the early days of the theater's operation vaudevillians would prepare for their performances. The legend claims that in the 1910s or 1920s, a fire fueled by the gas lamps that provided lighting before electricity ripped through the below-stage area, turning the concrete space into a giant oven, roasting the occupants inside and causing numerous deaths and horrific injuries. The damage some of the victims sustained was so severe that the bodies could not be fully recovered. During reconstruction

The San Jose Improv, located in the Jose Theatre building on Second Street. *Author photo*.

after the fire, concrete was simply poured over the bodies to form a new floor, leaving the dead entombed in the building to this day. Storytellers speculate that those poor souls who were never given a proper burial are responsible for the negative, oppressive energy and feelings of unease and discomfort many people report below the stage. It's a horrific story, but unfortunately for ghost hunters, it's not true. According to an article in the *San Jose Mercury News* from July 1989, the first fire in the building occurred in 1977, when an occult shop next door to the theater suffered a blaze that spread to the Jose and caused minor damage. This history is not widely known, as evidenced by the rumors that circulate today disguised as fact, and despite its ample storage space, the room below the stage remains unused, because no employees—including Williams, the manager—will go down there.

The upstairs bar area is another hot spot for paranormal activity with at least one aggressive entity that can't be explained away. In 2008, paranormal investigators captured an angry male voice in multiple EVPs, belligerently and profanely ordering the group out of the bar. Bartenders have reported that wine glasses stored over the bar rattle and clink together with no explanation. In an instance of an intelligent haunting, another EVP captures a woman's faint voice with a questioning tone in response to the investigators. Who these voices belong to, or what era they come from, is unknown. And it is likely to remain that way. Thousands of people have passed through and worked in the building, and any one of them could have left their energy or even their spirit behind to interact with the next generation of patrons, performers and employees. But from the different activity spread throughout the building, it seems the Improv has at least two distinct ghosts—one hostile, one playful—and possibly some residual energy that certain visitors are attuned to. The odds are good that an evening at the Improv will net you lots of laughs, some good food and drink and maybe even a ghost sighting.

6

PARKS

Santa Teresa Springs / Dottie's Pond

There's a wide swath of land in the southern hills of San Jose, a hidden gem that offers hiking, horseback riding, sweeping vistas and spine-tingling legends. Some sensitive souls can even feel the energetic vibrations from the land and seem attuned to the spirits that are said to have dwelled here for centuries.

In the 1800s, as the Mexican government declared independence from Spanish rule and took control of the territory of California, it decommissioned the Spanish missions and reallocated the large tracts of land the missions had occupied, granting them to Mexican citizens who had settled in the area. One of the better-known parcels in San Jose was the Bernal Grant, named Rancho Santa Teresa by its new owners, which spanned from Coyote Creek to the hills in the neighborhood we call Santa Teresa today. Deeded to José Joaquin Bernal in 1834 and passed to his descendants after his death, the land was eventually subdivided into suburban parcels and a large portion of it sold to the IBM corporation, which still maintains a research and development facility in the far southern reaches of Santa Teresa, east of Almaden. (See the Bernal Intermediate School section for more of the history of Bernal's settlement.)

Santa Teresa County Park sits within the former Bernal Grant, and it was a significant location for the Ohlone people, who lived in the area long before it was infiltrated by outsiders. These native people attributed their own mystical story to the land: that of a woman in black who offered healing powers to a tribe in need.

The legend says that members of the tribe living in the area became gravely ill. It could have been the result of an epidemic or from the cinnabar (from which mercury is extracted) with which they ceremonially painted their bodies. At any rate, tribal leaders were distressed about the frighteningly large number of their people falling ill and dying from the mysterious ailment. During an autumn feast, when various branches of the tribe came together for a yearly celebration, the leaders were discussing their concerns when, suddenly, the clear blue sky grew overcast and filled with dark, threatening clouds, blotting out the sun. The wind moaned and gusted around them, and lightning flashed in the sky above. From out of the storm clouds descended a beautiful woman dressed in black robes, emanating an aura of peace. She spoke in a low, soothing tone to the men, telling them that the greatest among them, Chief Umunhum, should draw the strongest, straightest arrow from his quiver and shoot it high into the sky. Wherever the arrow landed, the woman said, was where the tribe would find relief from their suffering.

As the rest of his people watched, Chief Umunhum selected his finest arrow, drew his bow and released the arrow skyward. All eyes followed its arc through the air and saw it land on a boulder on the side of a hill, splitting the boulder in two. From the break bubbled fresh, clear water, which the people rushed to drink, cupping their hands and filling their mouths again and again. The Ohlone people called the area 'Arma 'Ayttakis Rummey-tak, or "Place of the Spirit Woman Spring," and they stayed there, bathing in and drinking the cool, clean water until the illness that had plagued them gradually subsided, leaving them healthy once again.

The Ohlone developed a settlement near the spring. They remained in that location even as Spanish explorers arrived. When the land was deeded to Bernal and the family heard the legend of the Woman in Black, they decided the mysterious figure was really Saint Teresa of Avila, the Catholic patron saint of those who are ill. A shrine built in 1928 by Pedro Bernal, great-grandson of José Joaquin, in honor of Saint Teresa still exists at the site of the spring today.

Other versions of the story dispense with the deus ex machina appearance of the mysterious woman and simply have her place her hands on the stone, bringing forth water from a crack. But the heart of the story remains the same, and the Woman in Black is sometimes still seen today. Some have caught glimpses of her near the shrine, where the water trickles from the rocks, and she is a figure more peaceful than frightening but nonetheless mysterious. Her story is only one of the mystical tales told about the spring and the pond dug to hold its healing waters. This small body of water, known today as Dottie's Pond, is the setting for a love story gone murderously wrong—Romeo and Juliet with a parricidal twist.

According to one version of the legend, Dottie was a young woman who lived with her parents in a farmhouse on Bernal land. Some say they were part of the Bernal family. She was in love with a young man, but, as in the Shakespearean tragedy, her parents didn't approve of the relationship, and she was forbidden to see her paramour. Deciding to run away to be with her young lover, she was caught packing her belongings, and her father physically took his anger out on her, beating her violently. Incensed by her punishment, the girl channeled her rage into action and somehow summoned powers of telekinesis to hang her parents in the barn next to the house. She used the power of her mind to string them up by their necks until they were dead.

Then, out of grief or regret, or perhaps pulled by a force she couldn't control, the girl ran to the pond that now bears her name. Then, as now,

A barn at Bernal-Gulnac-Joice Ranch, where Dottie may have murdered her parents. *Author photo.*

it must have been dim and cool under the thick canopy of gnarled oak branches reaching over the pond, casting deep shadows across the water and on the vines sprawling over the ground. Was Dottie simply looking for relief beside the water that had healed so many before her? Or did she mean to wade into the pond and send herself deeper and deeper, trying to end her sorrow? We'll never know whether she intended to commit suicide or just cleanse herself of her guilt, because, the story goes, as Dottie flailed in the center of the pond, reeling from grief and trauma, a supernatural pair of giant hands rose out from the water and pulled her under, holding her down and drowning her. The hands are believed to have been sent from the devil, claiming this young murderess for himself. He traded her hell on earth for another, more permanent perdition.

Another telling of the story reports that Dottie first drowned herself in the pond, intentionally ending her life, and then her spirit returned to claim the lives of her parents, hanging them from the rafters in the barn in an act of vengeance from beyond the grave. But it seems her postmortem murders weren't enough to appease her, for today she targets hikers and anyone foolish enough to set foot in her pond, trying, perhaps, to punish them as she

Do ghostly hands lurk beneath the surface of Dottie's Pond in Santa Teresa County Park? *Author photo.*

was punished by her father. Savvy hikers know to stay securely on the other side of the railing from the pond, avoiding Dottie's wrath by not venturing too close to the dark waters.

And stories abound that Dottie—or the supernatural force that caused her demise—has never left. Today, visitors to the pond who arrive in the quiet of the morning or shortly before dusk claim to hear screams, cries for help they say are Dottie calling for mercy as she is pulled underwater to her death. The massive demon hands are said to lie in wait under the water, not disturbing the turtles who paddle guilelessly across the pond but instead biding their time until their next not-so-innocent victim comes along. A few daring souls, not trusting the legend and needing to test the limits for themselves, have attempted to wade into the pond and have needed to be rescued by friends after feeling that something is grabbing them from under the water. The ghost of Dottie has even been spotted near the pond, picking berries. The shadowy figure slips off into the brush before anyone can look too closely. She is perhaps replaying happier times on the ground she called home. Some people believe the nearby ranch house, occasionally open to the public, is where she was rumored to live with her parents, and one visitor to the park reported seeing the porch visibly shake when no one was in the home and when nothing else was shaking. It is a disturbance that might be attributed to the spirits of Dottie or her parents or to the strange energy that some feel permeates the land.

There are no records of a girl named Dottie or Dorothy ever living on the property or of any murders occurring on the land. We do know that José Joaquin Bernal had a granddaughter named Maria Dolores, possibly (though not likely) nicknamed Dottie, but she is confirmed to have married and died in the neighboring city of Santa Clara. The land belonged to and was worked by descendants of the Bernal family until 1980, when it was deeded to the county for public use, but there is no documentation or even speculation that the family was involved in such a grisly crime. But since Dottie's isn't the only supernatural story associated with the land, and since tales of spiritual events long predate European settlement, it seems entirely believable that the area does attract otherworldly energy. In any case, it's certainly an effective cautionary tale: Don't go swimming in strange bodies of water, and always listen to your parents. It pays to be careful, so make sure to keep your distance from the water's edge, lest you be the one Dottie decides to take down with her.

Almaden Winery Park

Residents of the Almaden Winery neighborhood in south San Jose enjoy luxury homes, scenic foothill views and an extraordinarily historic—and haunted—park almost literally in their front yards.

In 1852, the founder of the original Almaden Winery, Etienne Theé, a transplant from France, planted the first of what would become seventy-five acres of vineyards in the foothills of the Santa Cruz Mountains near Los Gatos, using seedlings he brought from his native Bordeaux. The Almaden Winery was the first commercial vineyard in Santa Clara County; the name *Almaden* came from the nearby New Almaden quicksilver mine. The winery was passed down to Theé's son-in-law Charles LeFranc in 1857. He in turn handed it to his son-in-law Paul Masson, builder of Mountain Winery in Saratoga. Through Prohibition, Masson sold the winery's grapes for juice to keep the business running and also produced and sold champagne under a license for "medicinal" purposes. In 1930, Masson sold the winery to the Almaden Vineyard Corporation, which increased production and distribution, making Almaden a well-known name among wine drinkers. In the late 1950s, the company left San Jose after falling victim to suburban sprawl.

Today, the street on the eastern edge of the park bears the name LeFranc Drive. The Friends of the Winemakers, a local nonprofit "dedicated to preserving the art and history of winemaking in the Santa Clara Valley," is working to establish a wine museum at the historic property. Unfortunately, all but two of the buildings on the estate were destroyed by fire in 1989, when workers using blowtorches in the cellar of one of the abandoned buildings ignited dry wood, sparking a five-alarm fire. The original winery building, dating from 1852 (some sources say 1859), was spared and still stands today, though it's behind a fence. The second building to escape a fiery demise was the old residence building, which now serves as a community center, available for party and event rentals. Several heritage California pepper trees also remain near the playgrounds and are said to mark the former driveway that led to the mansion on the estate. Though threatened by damage and potential demolition, the winery ultimately gained permanent recognition as a California State Historic Landmark.

But one of the original families associated with the winery didn't experience such a fortunate fate, suffering more than its fair share of tragedy and death. Charles LeFranc, son-in-law of the founder, was active and involved in day-to-day operations of the business until he was in his sixties. His life was

Above: The original Almaden
Winery building, dating from
the 1850s. *Author photo*.

Right: Heritage pepper trees
at Almaden Winery Park.
Author photo.

cut suddenly and tragically short in October 1877, when he was coming out from the cellar of the winery and caught sight of a team of runaway horses. He attempted to stop them but was trampled to death. A notice in the *Los Angeles Herald* cites both head and body injuries and "congestion of the brain" as the cause of death.

Charles's son Henry, who ran the winery with his brother-in-law Paul Masson, was also the victim of a tragic accident. In 1909, Henry and his wife were killed in what was described as a "horrible automobile-streetcar accident." The calamity occurred on August 19, 1909, at the intersection of Race and Park Avenues. Henry, his wife, Louise (nicknamed Neltie), and their three-year-old daughter, Delmas, also called Nelty, were in their automobile on the way out of town to visit friends. At the intersection, Henry's view was obstructed by a large barn on the corner, and he drove directly into the path of the interurban trolley that was trundling toward them at just under fifteen miles an hour. Some eyewitnesses claim that the LeFranc vehicle was speeding along at thirty-five miles per hour when it was struck by the electric streetcar, whose operator also had his view obstructed. Others reported that Henry, who was known as a careful driver, wasn't traveling above fifteen miles per hour. An article in the *San Francisco Examiner* on the day after the accident claimed it was "unavoidable." All three occupants were thrown from the car. Henry was killed instantly. Both Louise and Delmas struck their heads on the pavement as they landed. Louise was removed at once to the nearby O'Connor Sanitarium (precursor of the hospital of the same name) for medical treatment. Little Nelty, who was not initially thought to be injured, was taken to a nearby home but then sent to the sanitarium for her own treatment while her mother was undergoing an unsuccessful operation. Despite doctors having little hope of her recovery, and the newspaper headline claiming "Little Girl Is Dying," Nelty survived her injuries and lived to the age of seventy-one. She is buried at Oak Hill Memorial Park, reunited in death with her parents.

Today, some people report seeing at dusk and dawn a white shape seeming to emanate from the closed doors of the original winery building, a misty form that moves in a mass away from the doors, through the fence that surrounds the building and gradually fading away. One young woman who attempted a nighttime investigation with a group of friends told me that they had to call the excursion off shortly after their arrival at the park when one person in the group began exhibiting unnatural hysterical behavior that culminated in her becoming physically ill. She had never before felt such a violent reaction, and the witness who spoke to me told me she was sure that her friend was responding negatively to something in the environment, perhaps sensing an otherworldly entity that ended up driving her away.

Though some people who are drawn by a macabre fascination to Henry's story are eager to attribute the mysterious mist to his ghost, it's difficult—though not impossible—to believe that he would return in death to a location he had cut ties with nearly two decades before, as Paul Masson had bought out Henry's share of the business in 1892. It's much more likely that Henry LeFranc would haunt the location of his violent and tragic demise. Indeed, several houses along Park Avenue in the vicinity of the accident are said to be haunted. So it seems more plausible that the ghostly form at Almaden Winery Park is that of Charles LeFranc, emerging from the cellar after checking his vintage, replaying his last moments before he made the fateful decision to chase the horses that would end his life. And are the noises that sometimes sound like trucks rumbling down nearby Blossom Hill Road actually hoofbeats from the runaway team? Such an up-to-date corner of suburbia seems an unlikely setting for a residual haunting, but on a piece of land rooted in this rich history, anything's possible.

Alum Rock Park

On the northeastern edge of San Jose is a 720-acre city park that at one time drew visitors for its healing waters, recreational activities, miles of hiking trails and native flora and fauna. Alum Rock Park was created in 1872 as the city's first municipal park; the cultural history and the very geology of the land might contribute to the myriad legends and lore that speak of supernatural happenings in the area.

Like the rest of the terrain that makes up San Jose today, the area that would become Alum Rock Park was first inhabited by the Ohlone people, though the indigenous settlers here would have been a different faction than those who resided in other regions of the valley. After falling under Spanish, then Mexican, rule, the land became the property of the City of San Jose in 1851. It was first called the "Reservation" and sometimes "Penitencia Reservation," after Penitencia Creek, which flows through the canyon. The creek was where the Franciscan monks from the nearby missions went to pray for penance. Initially, a white powder found on a rock formation was thought to be alum, a mineral compound, and the name Alum Rock was applied in 1890 to the canyon that runs through the center of the park and, later, to the park as a whole. Eventually, scientists learned that the coating was actually a mix of sulfur, gypsum, thenardite and other minerals, but fortunately for posterity, the name Alum Rock was already well entrenched.

Once the city established ownership, it became clear that the land would lend itself to a variety of uses. Volcanic and seismic activity throughout the millennia—which we can thank for California's infamous earthquakes—helped carve out the natural canyon that contours the land, making it an appealing and scenic destination for hikers, picnickers and naturalists. To this day, long-dormant volcanoes continue to heat mineral water that burbles to the surface through fissures in the rock. Harnessing the perceived healing powers of these hot springs was the focus throughout most of the late nineteenth and early twentieth centuries. The earliest construction on the premises was a hotel and bathhouses, attracting visitors who were lured by the health benefits of the spa-like natural resource, and a narrow-gauge railroad served both tourists and locals. After a catastrophic flood in 1911 destroyed much of the existing infrastructure of the park, enterprising entrepreneurs undertook a building spree, constructing a natatorium, a new railroad line from downtown San Jose, a zoo (the remaining animals were moved in the 1970s to what would become Happy Hollow in Kelley Park), a restaurant and a bandstand.

The natatorium was an indoor swimming pool referred to as the "Plunge." It was forty-five feet wide by ninety feet long. In her blog *Alum Rock Park History*, Judy Thompson writes: "It was a wondrous building which stood on the site of today's service yard near the visitors' center. It had the character of a World's Fair conservatory, roofed over by a large vaulted ceiling with skylights running its length. Inside, on the side walls, were high galleries from which observers could watch the daring antics going on below." It also featured a two-story-high water slide that audacious swimmers would fly down headfirst. Shockingly, no deaths were reported at the pool.

One of the more remarkable—and, it turns out, fraudulent—attractions at the park in the early twentieth century was the Alum Rock Meteor, a huge chunk of rock near the Penitencia Creek entrance estimated by its promoters to weigh over 2,000 tons. Trains into the park would stop here by request for visitors to marvel at the mysterious boulder, and old-timers in the neighborhood, some who had lived through the Spanish and Mexican governments, swore that they had witnessed its blazing descent from the night sky. Despite repeated declarations from scientists at the time that it was

The misnamed Alum Rock meteor. *1900, San Jose, Alum Rock Park meteor. Courtesy of San Jose Public Library, California Room, Clyde Arbuckle Photograph Collection.*

not, in fact, a meteorite, the boulder was a major tourist draw. Many people were shocked when, in 1918, it was discovered that the "space rock" weighed just 389 tons and was mainly composed of manganese, an earthly element. The boulder was mined for its manganese ore to assist in the war effort, and even though it's no longer extant, the legend surrounding it has persisted. Some still associate Alum Rock Park with otherworldly or extraterrestrial phenomena, believing, perhaps, that some alien life-form hitched a ride on the meteor as it fell from space. (Never mind that it didn't.)

Ironically, the natural and man-made attractions that made the park so popular were responsible for its decline. At its height, nearly ten thousand visitors would arrive at the park on some Sundays. With the majority of its attractions concentrated on the floor of the canyon, the influx of sightseers soon caused unintended destruction of native plant and animal life. Those wishing to enjoy unspoiled nature stopped coming. As the site emptied of visitors, it became frequented by unsavory characters conducting nefarious or criminal activity, though reports of crime in the park may have been exaggerated. Perhaps undeservedly, the park acquired a reputation as a dangerous and forbidding place, which may still fuel stories of negative spiritual energy.

Many records surrounding the park and the enterprises that once operated within its bounds have been lost to time, but we do know that throughout its long history there have been misfortunes, accidents and a number of deaths. These could offer clues to the claims of hauntings. The hotel burned to the ground in 1890 under mysterious circumstances, though no lives were lost. Two separate railway accidents, in 1903 and 1909, were responsible for the deaths of at least four people. The first occurred when a train car began to roll down a slight grade as passengers were boarding it. The conductor, unable to stop the car as it gathered momentum, watched in horror as the car crashed before a tight turn, sending passengers flying into the air. Two adults and a young girl died of their injuries. The latter accident was even more horrific. A fifteen-year-old boy, sticking his head out of the train window as it went through a tunnel, came to a grisly end when he was decapitated. The park is not immune from present-day tragedies, either. Every couple of years, another person meets their death at the park, from an accident, an act of violence or by their own hand. Ghost sightings specific to these deaths have not been reported, but these victims may very well be responsible for the persistent feelings of unease that both repel and attract some visitors.

The flowing waters of Penitencia Creek have fueled sightings of La Llorona, the weeping mother familiar in Mexican folklore who searches for her dead children. There is also a legend that a remote and inaccessible cave was the hiding place of Joaquín Murrieta, the legendary bandit mythologized by some as a gold rush–era Robin Hood. Rumors claim that Murrieta hid in the park while on the run from law enforcement; some stories hold that he stashed treasure in the cave that no one has ever found.

The most lurid and outrageous supernatural story is that a compound of cannibalistic albinos, possibly undead, is located in the hills. The beings lurk around the log cabin at the center of the park, appearing from the shadows to accost oblivious hikers and, gruesomely, feed on the canine population of the neighborhood. For unexplained reasons, San Jose has more than its share of urban legends featuring albinos, to the growing consternation of those who are troubled by the vilifying of this population. It's not likely that this legend will be laid to rest anytime soon, but perhaps it's time to remove any reference to skin pigmentation and focus more on other aspects of these likely fictional hill dwellers, such as their supposed predilection for feasting on poodle meat.

A stone bridge crosses Penitencia Creek in Alum Rock Park. *Author photo*.

The bubbling water that was once so popular an attraction for visitors to the park might also hold the key to the park's paranormal reputation. Sulfur and other minerals dissolve in the hot water as it flows up through the ground, resulting in a distinctive sulfurous odor that calls to mind fire and brimstone. Some superstitious souls suspect that this water is the devil's own liquid. Many who have unwisely tasted the sulfur-tinged water might well believe they've sipped Satan's brew. With the park's share of misfortune and tragedy, perhaps these sensitive souls are right that there are darker, even devilish forces at play.

Running water may act as a source of energy for the manifestation of paranormal activity. Some in the paranormal field also believe that fault lines can fuel ghostly goings-on. The internal stress along seismic fault lines can build up into magnetic fields that lie just under the earth's surface, acting as a battery for spirits to manifest, and Alum Rock Canyon is crossed by the active Calaveras Fault. Additionally, certain types of rocks such as sandstone and limestone are said to "store" historical energy, like a memory bank for past events on the land. The information can be released as a residual haunting or the replaying of a historical event. Alum Rock Park contains large quantities of sandstone, much of which has been lifted to near the surface from underlying seismic activity. With this confluence of running water, a fault zone and memory-capable rock, Alum Rock Park seems to have the perfect characteristics for hauntings to occur.

After its decline, city officials decided to return the park to its more natural state, pulling down most of the garish amusement park structures and restoring natural habitats. While some residents bemoan what they perceive as the city's lack of historical appreciation, the flora and fauna of the park have flourished as a result of these conservation efforts, and those who visit now are rewarded with increased sightings of birds, insects, animals and plants. The luckiest of visitors might even spot a ghost.

7
ROADS

SAN FELIPE ROAD

San Felipe Road—long, twisting and deadly—runs for miles through southeast San Jose. The Silver Creek area, where the road begins, is densely populated and suburban. However, as the road winds past the country club and climbs the foothills of Mount Hamilton, it becomes rural, isolated, narrow and sinister. Streetlights are few and far between, eucalyptus trees stand like ancient sentinels at the road's edge and, at night, the darkness completely encompasses the road and seems impermeable beyond the reach of a car's headlights. There have long been reports of strange happenings in these hills, including violent acts and terrifying apparitions.

Most of the stories revolve around the one-room schoolhouse, known as the Highland School, that stood in the San Felipe Valley, south of San Jose. In a photo dating from 1876, sixteen children and their male teacher stand in front of the white clapboard structure, the girls on one side of the front steps and the boys on the other. The teacher holds a tall hat in his hands. The children look stiff yet tidy. The building is neatly painted, a respectable place for children of the valley to earn their grammar school education.

Despite the orderly appearance, events surrounding the school weren't always so placid, according to legend. At some undisclosed point in time after that photo was taken, when a female teacher was mistress of the school, tragedy struck. The teacher, long unhappy in her marriage,

Legends of San Felipe Road include a murderous schoolteacher and a disappearing white van. *Author photo.*

reached the end of her rope one day and took her anger and frustration out on her students, methodically murdering them one by one as they arrived at school for the day. Supposedly, she hanged them in a barn near the schoolhouse. People who have been near the schoolhouse at night report hearing bloodcurdling cries of children coming from inside. This is disturbing on its own, but it is even more horrifying considering that the building has been abandoned for decades.

The murders and the hauntings are unconfirmed and are likely to remain that way, as the schoolhouse now sits on private property. That portion of San Felipe Road is also private and is blocked by a gate across the road. Potential ghost hunters would do well to respect the laws and the privacy of the people who live on this road.

There's more to fear from this road beyond agitated residents and trespassing violations. Nearly everyone who has driven here at night has an eerie story to tell. If you watch your rearview mirror, you might see something moving behind your car, a shadowy figure that seems to come out of the darkness. But if you turn around to look, there won't be anything there. There are also consistent reports of a white van chasing cars back toward town. The van materializes out of nowhere and then disappears as quickly as it appeared. While this might be easily explained as a security vehicle hired by residents to patrol their private property, it doesn't explain how the van seems to vanish without a trace. The most frightening claim comes from people who have checked their cars after returning home from their midnight drives. Even if they make it down San Felipe Road and back with no other spooky occurrences, many people claim to find white handprints on the outside of their car, as if someone—or something—had been riding along with them, trying to get in.

There is one last note to make about San Felipe Road. While claims of murder and ghosts are not documented, the number of car crashes that have occurred on this road are. Fatal accidents are a nearly annual event, and it's highly unlikely that the paranormal has anything to do with them. More likely it's a combination of a winding road, near isolation and thrill-seeking drivers. Practice caution if you explore this area of town, or the next ghost people claim to see could be yours.

Quimby Road

One of San Jose's oldest roads happens to be one of its most remote and rural. Its name pays homage to a man who was present in San Jose during the days of California's founding and who played a pivotal role in the physical development of the city. His legacy is visible today in the streets of downtown. His namesake road is haunted by one of San Jose's most persistent urban legends, that of the Quimby Road Jogger.

John Alonzo Quimby (also spelled Quinby in contemporaneous documents) was a prominent local citizen present at the first state legislature of California, held in San Jose from December 1849 to April 1850. Intriguingly enough, this legislature has its own ghost story. At the dawn of California's statehood, sixteen senators representing the nine districts established by the Mexican government were tasked with creating the first state constitution and seating San Jose as the state capital. While the members of the assembly were highly effective in using their limited political experience to draft complex laws, some of which are still in place today, they also earned the sobriquet "Legislature of a Thousand Drinks." The origin for this nickname lies with Senator Thomas Jefferson Green, by all accounts a hard-drinking carouser who, after each session, invited his colleagues to "have a drink—have a thousand drinks." Some historians decry the nickname as apocryphal and undeserved, and by many accounts Green's productive peers didn't share his penchant for booze. Historian James Scherer wrote, "The title coterie that [Senator Green] gathered about him had no influence upon the working members" of the legislature. But the nickname stuck, and the phrase is written on a plaque commemorating the site of the first capital of California, located in what is now the Circle of Palms Plaza on Market Street. Some late-night visitors to the Circle of Palms and Plaza de Cesar Chavez, across the street, claim to hear the ghostly reverberation of a boisterous gathering. The rousing cheers and clinking glasses are often attributed to Green and his inebriate cronies celebrating another successful day of politicking. They're especially high-spirited on cold December nights.

Despite the rumored festivities at the legislature, J.A. Quimby wasn't derailed by Green's antics. Quimby embarked on an impressive and successful record of public service. He served in the California state legislature, as mayor of San Jose (1863–69) and on the Board of County Supervisors. In this latter role, he focused on the physical and economic growth of downtown San Jose, encouraging development and expansion outward from the intersection of Market and Santa Clara Streets by selling small parcels of land and instituting the infrastructure and utilities needed to sustain them. During Quimby's tenure as a county supervisor, the agricultural industry of the Santa Clara Valley flourished, the state took over management of the college now known as San Jose State University and the first public transit system in the city—a precursor of today's light-rail system—was established.

Quimby's second home, where he lived when he wasn't working downtown, was a farm in the Evergreen region near the eastern foothills. The road that bears his name was established in the 1860s or 1870s and was used to reach Mount Hamilton Road, built to access the Lick Observatory at the summit of Mount Hamilton. Quimby Road today begins at Eastridge Mall and is a major corridor through east San Jose, passing by schools, shops and houses until east of Murillo Avenue, when the suburban sprawl changes as the road ascends the foothills. The road narrows, the shoulder virtually disappears and, in places, no guardrail protects the westbound lane from an ever-increasing drop-off. It is not for the distracted or inexperienced driver or for the faint of heart—for more than one reason. This is where most of the sightings of the reclusive phantom occur.

The legend passed down about this long and winding road is made all the more intriguing by its vagueness. A spectral jogger is said to run along the road in the dark of night. Most often seen by motorists and passersby close to midnight, the ghostly jogger veers off the side of the road when anyone comes too close, disappearing into the bushes and vanishing from sight. Some witnesses claim that the jogger is missing its head, a truly terrifying apparition. Hikers on the Heron Trail have also laid claim to the jogger. This trail runs through Joseph D. Grant County Park in the eastern hills and intersects Quimby Road just west of where Quimby ends at Mount Hamilton Road. An online source states that some hikers who came face-to-face with the ghost reported feeling as if it peered directly into their souls before turning and running off. Apparently, this is the version of the ghost that retains its head. The apparition leaves the witnesses shaking with fright and, in some cases, physically ill, as though in the grips of a terrible fever.

Drivers on Quimby Road may spot the notorious midnight jogger. *Author photo.*

Even without a potentially decapitated spirit terrifying those who confront it, this is a dangerous stretch of road. Narrow, winding and isolated, it attracts thrill-seeking drivers who are willing to flout any traffic laws. Several deaths of cyclists, pedestrians and motorists are associated with Quimby Road, but the story of the ghostly jogger seems to predate the rash of deaths validated by news reports. Who the jogger was and why his spirit chose this particular road remain unknown. What we do know is that it prefers to run alone.

HICKS ROAD

No thoroughfare strikes more fear into the hearts of native San Joseans—especially those who grew up or went to school in the Almaden Valley—than Hicks Road. A winding, eight-mile drive through the foothills of the Santa Cruz Mountains, Hicks Road runs roughly northwest to southeast from Camden Avenue to Alamitos Road. Amid suburban sprawl and development encroaching on one of the last few wild spaces within the city limits, Hicks Road straddles the line between residential and rural, easily accessed from nearby neighborhoods yet seemingly remote and removed from civilization. The road offers access to a county park and regional open space preserve and is also the most accessible route to Mount Umunhum Road, which served the U.S. Air Force radar station at the top of the mountain. The station was active at the height of the Cold War. A number of houses are found on this road as well.

Hicks Road is a popular destination for local teens to take their newly minted driver's licenses and parents' cars out for a spin. It's also rumored to be an ideal place to hide dead bodies, and it's the setting for a number of legends and scary stories that make the rounds of area high schools. But there is one element above all others for which Hicks Road is known: the albinos.

Before investigating the legend, it's worth asserting that any persecution of or superstitious thinking about people with albinism is outdated, offensive and erroneous. Because this is the primary claim surrounding Hicks Road, we will look briefly at what tales are told while remembering that these stories originated in a time that often demonized the "other." What follows is a completely fictional description that reads uncomfortably today in its oppression and exploitation of those with albinism.

For generations, stories have abounded about the enclave of reclusive, violent and possibly supernatural people—if they are indeed human—who terrorize these hills, and the most enduring part of the legend lies in their physical description. They are said to possess pallid white skin and glowing red eyes, earning them the moniker "blood albinos." With this adjective, a subtle yet critical difference, this group is distinguished from the clans of non-blood albinos said to live near Uvas Reservoir, the Cats Restaurant on Highway 17, Alum Rock Park, Mount Hamilton Road and Marsh Road in Milpitas. According to a theory popularized by a local psychic, the albinos are actually the ghosts of a territorial tribe of people (never specifically identified as, but assumed to be, Native Americans, which is problematic in its own way) that remain on the land they once occupied. The hypothesis

Hicks Road is one of San Jose's best-known haunted locations. *Author photo.*

is that they are composed of ectoplasm, which may give a bloodless, white appearance. Other scenarios posit the contingent as the last of a dying race of aliens or a genetically mutated group of squatters suffering from mercury poisoning from the nearby quicksilver mines.

While this is a precise and evocative description that probably adds to the shocking nature of the story, we must disregard any melanin-related claims in the lore and focus on the actions of these mythical individuals, especially the cult-like nature of their existence in the hills.

One thing many people can agree on is that this sect has cannibalistic tendencies and a predilection for human blood, preying on unfortunate local drivers and explorers who unwittingly stumble into the black rituals they perform under cover of darkness. At the very least, they desire the blood of roadkill or other wild animals they can hunt and feast on, especially the deer and mountain lions that run rampant in this corner of San Jose. Another consistent claim is that they emit shrill, bloodcurdling screams that can be heard echoing for miles throughout the hills and among the oak trees. Like those who hear the Sirens of Greek mythology, unfortunate witnesses to these supernatural shrieks are said to be driven insane and compelled to their doom, especially if they are literally driving at the time. Often, the result is a car accident or mental anguish that persists even after the witness returns to civilization. One detail that often goes unreported is that the denizens of the enclave are toeless, although perhaps this is one of the physical mutations they are said to exhibit.

Some versions of the story have the clan escaping from a now-abandoned insane asylum, supposedly called Cinnabar Hills, that is said to have existed in the hills beyond New Almaden; a few disreputable internet sources even claim to have directions to the lost asylum. However, while certainly creepy, this allegation can be put to rest as patently false, according to local historians, the memories of longtime residents and all available documentation, including city and county records. This asylum never existed and is in fact a completely fictional invention.

Reports of paranormal or otherworldly activity on the road are vague, as urban legends sometimes are, but also unnerving in their simplicity. People who park their cars along the road and get out to explore sometimes report one or more human-like figures suddenly appearing nearby in the woods, standing motionless, staring at them with an intensity that makes the would-be adventurers quickly return to the safety of their automobiles. At times, the figures are clothed in black robes; often, they are too indistinct to determine what they're wearing or even if they're human. Sometimes, they attempt to chase, either singly or in groups, trespassers. Many drivers who traverse the road at night claim their headlights illuminate glowing eyes lurking in the darkness just off the edge of the road. One story reports that if you stop near the Wood Road intersection, members of the clan will leap out of the roadside brush and attempt to pull you out of your car. Another active landmark is the Guadalupe Reservoir. Foolhardy investigators who go off-trail looking for ghouls report seeing shadowy figures watching from across the water.

The misanthropic clan members that inhabit the hills are not the only specters to haunt this road. There are pervasive reports of phantom headlights that come head-on toward drivers and suddenly disappear, with no other vehicles in sight. A white pickup truck is said to chase people off the road and then mysteriously vanish. Yet another tale involves the "Devil's Door," a large boulder with a door painted on it. Local teenagers dare each other to knock three times on the door to see if the devil himself will

Shadowy figures have been seen across the water of the Guadalupe Reservoir. *Author photo*.

answer. The devil also seems to have possession of a bridge at an undisclosed location along the road. If a person's name is carved into the cursed bridge, that person will die.

The intersection of Shannon and Hicks Roads features the ghost of an elderly woman wandering on the roadside, appearing lost and disoriented. If motorists pull over and offer the ghost a ride, it will accept, but it disappears before getting into the car.

Hicks Road even has its own classic phantom hitchhiker. The story goes that a woman in a bloody white dress wanders the road at night; as you pass her and keep driving, she appears again and again ahead of you as you round each new bend in the road. The longer she is ignored, the angrier she becomes, until motorists find her standing in the middle of the road before them. Unable to stop, they might run right through her, their cars continuing on without disturbance—until the occupants hear her clinging to the top of their car or speeding along with them outside a passenger window. There is one story of a driver who demonstrated compassion and stopped to pick her up, offering her a ride home and giving her his leather jacket to wear against the frigid night air. The sympathetic driver dropped her off at her home, located just past New Almaden. When he returned to pick up his jacket the next day, he was told by a resident of the house that the hitchhiking woman was a sister (in some versions a daughter) who died (or disappeared) and was marked by a memorial stone at Oak Hill cemetery. When the driver visited the cemetery for himself, he found his jacket folded neatly on top of the woman's headstone.

One final tale is said to originate from a bicyclist who was killed on the road when he was tragically hit by a car. He now appears as a ghost rider only visible in a car's mirrors as it drives down the road. The most bizarre thing about this spectral cyclist is that he wears a trench coat and rides a bicycle with no wheels. This is a popular, albeit dangerous, road for cyclists, and there are several recorded deaths from both solo bicycle accidents and car crashes, though it's impossible to attribute this spirit to any victim in particular.

A 2009 short film is inspired by the legend, but stories of the colony in this area date to at least the 1960s. One resident who was in high school during that decade has distinct memories of classmates exploring Hicks Road as a rite of passage. Where did the legend come from? An online commenter posted on a forum about the urban legend: "Years ago I met one of the previous owners of the Quicksilver mines. When they found roadkill, they would place it at the entrances of open mines to scare people from going in. My guess is the albino story became an extension from that." It's also possible, as some have speculated, that employees of the U.S. Air Force station on top of Mount Umunhum encouraged or even fabricated the stories to deter curious explorers who might inadvertently stumble onto military property. Likewise, those who engaged in illegal activity, possibly drug-related, might also have wished to discourage visitors to these hills. The origins will never be confirmed, but the paranormal stories, rife with accounts of reckless behavior and disastrous consequences, can be read as cautionary tales, especially for bored teenagers who seem the most drawn to this remote area.

By all accounts, residents in this secluded pocket of San Jose have no desire to be disturbed. Historically, many people have reported unpleasant run-ins with locals who take umbrage with trespassing. To preserve the peace and safety of all involved, the best way to investigate this lore is through reading stories about it, and if you do choose to explore in person, abide by laws and common sense. As long as there are teenagers growing up in San Jose, there will be urban legends about and midnight drives along Hicks Road—even if there aren't albinos.

8

New Almaden

The mid-1800s in California are most often associated with the gold rush, but in the area south of San Jose proper known as New Almaden, cinnabar, the ore that contains the liquid metal mercury, was the local hot commodity. The ore was utilized by the native Ohlone people for trading and religious ceremonies and as body paint, and it was recognized as a precious metal by Mexican artillery officer Andrés Castillera. Reports of the abundance of the ore in the green hills of New Almaden soon drew miners to the little community from near and far in their own rush to stake their claims and make their fortunes.

At its most populous, nearly three thousand people lived in New Almaden. Management and furnace workers resided in the Hacienda area, which was the center of the town. Most of the miners lived in Spanishtown and Englishtown, separate villages built into the hillsides above the mining tunnels. Even after the gold rush ended in the 1850s and mercury was no longer needed to help extract gold from sediment, the New Almaden mines saw several resurgences in industry through the end of World War II, though unused buildings on the hillsides were removed by the Civilian Conservation Corps in the 1930s. In 1976, the Santa Clara County Board of Supervisors purchased the site of the former mines for use as a county park. Today, a handful of people lives in this small, tightly-knit community, residing in the original homes of mining company officials and their families, alongside the ghosts that never left New Almaden.

LA FORÊT RESTAURANT

In 1848, after the initial cinnabar discovery and before the population boom that led to impressive census numbers, a two-story building was constructed near Alamitos Creek to house the growing number of miners flocking to the area. This was the first two-story hotel in California, and not only did it offer workingmen a comfortable place to sleep, it also served hot meals in the dining room downstairs. The original building burned in 1875 and was rebuilt as the wood structure that stands now. After its incarnation as a boardinghouse ended in 1912, it was vacant for many years. It then reopened as various restaurants, including the popular Cafe del Rio in the 1930s and La Forêt in 1980. The white, two-story clapboard building is now a world away from its rustic roots as a miners' hostel. Neat brick borders enclose landscaping out front, and next to the front door, steps descend to a creekside patio, illuminated in the evenings by overhead string lights. Inside, a foyer with dark velvet chairs leads into small dining rooms, intimately nestled together, with elegant, dark red walls and dim, romantic lighting. Walls of windows overlook the trees outside.

The building that now houses La Forêt was once a boardinghouse for miners. *Author photo.*

Despite the changes of ownership and periods when the building stood empty, it appears that some spirits have remained. Patrons and employees of La Forêt frequently report the indistinct figure of a woman moving through the dining rooms just before the restaurant closes for the evening. Witnesses say she floats, not walks, between the tables and is dressed in nineteenth-century clothing. She's about five feet tall with curly gray hair and hazel eyes and hands that look slightly deformed as if by arthritis. She seems pleased with what she sees, as if she approves of how the restaurant is being run. Some speculate she's the ghost of a former owner or manager of the restaurant.

There are indications that additional, more mischievous spirits might be in the building. People feel cool breezes when there's no explanation; napkins are rearranged on tables; and silverware will fall when no one is around. On the second floor, ghosts of miners who formerly lived there are sometimes seen, dirty and bearded. Perhaps the miners died in their rooms, or their spirits are drawn back to a place where they felt some creature comforts after their physical toil in the mines. The building's proximity to the running water of Alamitos Creek adds not only a romantic atmosphere to the restaurant but also may allow the spirits to more easily manifest. However they appear, and whoever they are, the ghosts of La Forêt are one more link to the rich history that feels almost tangible in New Almaden today.

HACIENDA CEMETERY

Hacienda Cemetery is the eternal home to some New Almaden residents, both miners and prominent community members, from the late 1800s to the early 1900s. The cemetery, dating to the early 1850s, is thought to be the final resting place of about fifty people; today, due to age and vandalism, a number of the graves are unmarked. In 1928, a musician named Ben Black bought some of the land owned by the mining company near the Hacienda and attempted to subdivide it: when he couldn't get the necessary permits to extend Bertram Road through the cemetery, he took matters into his own hands, piloting a bulldozer in the middle of the night and cutting a swath directly through the cemetery and over a number of occupied graves. Today, the cemetery is divided in two, on either side of the road, and it's said that when you drive down that road, the bumps you pass over are graves. In 1974, the cemetery was deeded to the California Pioneers of Santa Clara

Above: Hacienda Cemetery on Bertram Road. *Author photo.*

Left: The final resting place of Bert Barrett's arm. *Author photo.*

County, under whose care (along with that of neighborhood volunteers) it remains today.

Vandalism and bodies under the roadway aren't the only unfortunate elements associated with this tiny cemetery. Bertram Road, the narrow lane that runs on the south side of Alamitos Creek, parallel to Almaden Road behind the mining museum and Casa Grande, is named after Richard Bertram Barrett, also called Bert. At the age of thirteen, Bert lost his left arm in a hunting accident. In accordance with laws and custom of the time, his arm was required to be given a proper burial and thus was interred in Hacienda Cemetery. At the grave, a wooden marker, surrounded by a white picket fence, reads, "Richard Bertram 'Bert' Barrett. His arm lies here. 1893. May it rest in peace."

Bert himself lived for another sixty-six years, working as chief sanitation engineer for Santa Clara County and passing away in 1957. The rest of his body, sans left arm, is interred in Oak Hill Memorial Park, eleven miles away from New Almaden, where he rests peacefully. But what of that arm?

Legend has it that, on Halloween night and other evenings when the moon is full, the arm of Bert Barrett comes back to life and crawls out of its lonely grave, clawing its way across the ground in search of the rest of its body. Its fingers scramble to find purchase in the dirt, and it scales the picket fence with the ease of a thirteen-year-old boy. Using the light of the moon to guide its path, the disembodied limb tries to steer a course down the hilly lanes of New Almaden, perhaps hoping to reanimate the rest of its corpse when it finds it.

The Barretts' rented home—which may have notification of possible paranormal activity written into its property deed, as do selected houses along this road—is across Alamitos Creek from the cemetery and is known as Cottage Number Five or the Hauck Residence, after the treasurer of the New Almaden company from 1915 to 1930. While the home doesn't seem to have any legends associated with it, it's not difficult to imagine Bert Barrett's disembodied arm stopping by its old home on its jaunt down the road to Oak Hill cemetery in San Jose.

Another dwelling that does have a legend is the former home of Mary Ellen Pleasant, a fascinating woman who is more closely associated with San Francisco but who nevertheless has roots in San Jose. Mary Pleasant, a freed slave, abolitionist and silent business partner of Thomas Bell, an investor in the mines, lived in New Almaden in the 1860s. Rumor has it that she operated a brothel for the miners, possibly out of the large house known as Casa Grande, and that her house, across Alamitos Creek from the cemetery, was used as an abortion clinic. Some believe the unborn children still haunt the house. Throughout her life, Mary Ellen was also rumored (though probably unfairly) to be a voodoo practitioner. At the death of Thomas Bell, who lived with his wife in Mary Ellen's San Francisco home, it's said that she was found to be "pulling apart the bones of his head and picking out bits of his brain." It's a vile scenario, to be sure, and one that only adds to the mystery and obfuscation of her life and lends even more chilling plausibility to the possibility that her former home on Almaden Road is haunted.

While all this may be the stuff of campfire tales and spooky stories told in the dark, all it takes is one visit to New Almaden to believe that the legends are true. Despite the best efforts of volunteers to maintain the cemetery on Bertram Road, nature has continued to take its course, with old oak trees spreading their canopies overhead and vinca vines choking the ground underfoot. According to Kitty Monahan, longtime resident of New Almaden and president of the New Almaden Quicksilver County Park Association, at one time the cemetery was larger than its current boundaries. So, in addition to the bodies under the road, there are most likely more graves lost to time under the nearby homes, leading to the likelihood of a number of haunted houses. Also, the creek that runs alongside the cemetery would occasionally flood, sending water up the riverbank toward the cemetery and unmooring bodies from the earth and floating them downstream, a problem eventually mitigated by the U.S. Army Corps of Engineers. Anywhere that bodies are disturbed is prime stomping ground for restless spirits, and the dead haven't always rested peacefully in New Almaden.

9

PRIVATE HOMES

PARK AVENUE

Park Avenue runs from Plaza de Cesar Chavez in the heart of downtown San Jose to Santa Clara University. Along the way, it passes other icons of the city such as the Tech Interactive, technology giant Adobe Inc., the 1930s-era Hoover Middle School and the extensive and unique Rosicrucian Egyptian Museum, interspersed with plenty of private residences. A number of these homes were built before the turn of the twentieth century on land that was part of the original Rancho Los Coches land grant owned by Antonio Suñol. Many of them may be home to more than just the living who reside in them.

It's in one of these old Victorians, with its gingerbread trim and carefully restored original paint colors, that the current homeowner, Marilyn, has had nearly constant paranormal experiences. The original house on the property, which is near Lincoln Avenue, was built in 1896. It was one of the first homes to be built on Park Avenue, in an area predominated by wheat fields. A creek ran across what became the front of the property, the area of the driveway today. Running water is said to be a conduit for paranormal activity, attracting and retaining spiritual energy. Perhaps this is why Marilyn and others have experienced ghosts for nearly a century.

According to Marilyn, the 1896 residence was owned by a family named Van Dyke. They rebuilt it in 1906, and this is the house that stands today. (There's no information on whether or not the rebuild was necessary after

This Victorian home on Park Avenue dates from 1896. *Author photo.*

the earthquake of 1906.) Two children in the family passed away in the home in 1918 during the Spanish flu epidemic. The daughter was sixteen; the son was eight. Marilyn believes they never left.

A teenage girl with blonde hair and wearing a white dressing gown passes through the kitchen, appearing at one end of the room and walking straight through the closed door to the outside. Marilyn has seen her countless times; her partner, Stefen, has seen the girl as well and reported that the first time he saw her, she appeared so real that he wondered why there was someone else in their home. "She didn't even look at me," Stefen says; she just walked past him as though he wasn't there. This lends support to the idea that she is a residual haunting, or a place memory, a spirit performing actions she carried out when she was alive, almost as a tape recorder playing back a recording from long ago. There's no awareness or interaction, just a memory stamped in time and space that's visible to us today. "I never even believed in ghosts till I moved here six years ago," Stefen says. "I didn't believe in it till I saw that."

Another spirit in the house seems to have a consciousness that suggests an intelligent haunting. A young boy around the age of eight (the same age as the Van Dyke son who perished from influenza) with brown hair and wearing a white shirt with a drawstring neckline is often seen at the top of the stairs, peeking down at the first floor through the spindles. You can see right through him, and he appears to notice when people are looking at him. The same boy is seen running halfway down the stairs, then back up, or moving along the upstairs hallway. Sometimes, when people are downstairs and no one is on the second floor, they hear noises from above, as if a child is jumping off of a bed and running along the floor.

The next owners after the Van Dyke family were the parents of Marilyn's late husband. They bought the house around 1930. Her mother-in-law, Marilyn says, heard whispering when she was alone in the house and was sometimes so frightened at how loud it was that she had to leave. When Marilyn and her husband, Henry, inherited the property in 1975, they, too, were immediately witness to whatever was in the house, although Marilyn says it never scared her. "I'm used to ghosts," she says. And she has an agreement with the spirits in the home: they won't hurt her or her loved ones, and she'll leave them be.

Despite the agreement, the spirits are sometimes a little too personal for comfort for some. Marilyn hears a man speaking in Portuguese; she believes it's the landowner who sold the property to the Van Dykes. She recorded a man's voice outside her home calling her "doña," or great lady of the house, and she has felt a hand stroking her hair.

The drawing on the wall, found under the wallpaper. Her ghost has been seen in the house. *Courtesy of Marilyn Jerkovich.*

She also believes her late husband is in the home, though he did not pass away there; she hears his voice calling her "honey" and smells his scent. The final spirit she's seen, although she doesn't know who it is, is an old woman who, off and on for twenty years, leaned against the doorjamb in Marilyn's bedroom upstairs. Marilyn would wake in the night to see her standing there. Years later, while stripping layers of wallpaper from that bedroom wall , she came across a drawing on the wall, a sketch of an elderly woman's face. It was the same face Marilyn had seen on the woman standing in her doorway.

With all of these ghostly encounters, history is palpable in the house on Park Avenue. Living in a home that still contains the energy from those who used to reside there—and indeed died there—may be unsettling to some, but Marilyn seems to treasure her experiences with the ghosts. Stefen, who often hears the voice of a man speaking to him in the garage behind the house, agrees, calling the spirits "very pleasant." That's quite the endorsement coming from a skeptic turned believer.

HELLYER HOUSE

The center of hell—on the east side of San Jose? That's the story believed by many residents who have driven past the legendary house on the northeast corner of Hellyer Avenue and Senter Road. The house itself is unremarkable; like many others on the street, it's a single-story structure with nested gables, painted light blue with a strikingly bright blue front door. The front yard is completely paved, and the whole front of the property is surrounded by a black iron fence with pointed finial tips, a decidedly unwelcome touch. At one point, a small American flag appeared in the front window, and from time to time a car has been seen pulling into and out of the garage. But apart from the motion-activated lights and security cameras mounted on the exterior, the house offers no signs of life.

There are several stories associated with the property, each one lacking details that could lend credence to the claims, but each story is consistently centered on violent deaths, attempts to cleanse the house of evil spirits and a forlorn entity that has never left.

According to city property records, the house was built in 1988 and sold in 1989. At some point in those early years, the first story reports, a teenage girl was living in the house with her parents. She became pregnant, much to the dismay and disappointment of her conservative family, and after a

The infamous Hellyer House. *Author photo.*

vicious argument in which they threatened to disown her, she ended up murdering her parents and then hanging herself in the garage. Subsequent occupants reported constant unexplained noise coming from the house at all hours, including the distressing sounds of a girl crying, with the activity most prevalent in the garage.

An alternate version that contains elements of the previous story involves a family of three: mother, daughter and son. One evening, the mother and son got into such a violent argument that the son ended up killing the mother and then himself. The teenage daughter, hysterical with shock and grief, called 911, but before police could arrive, she hauled herself out to the garage, where she hanged herself from the rafters and joined her family in death.

In a third, lesser-reported but still circulating tale about the house, a teacher at a nearby school murdered his wife and tried to blame her death on an intruder. His cover-up failed, and he was tried and convicted of her murder. While disturbing to think that someone in such an esteemed profession would commit such a heinous act, there are no records or documents to verify this story, and it seems the least likely of the three to have occurred.

But no matter who the victims were or what caused their deaths, a persistent element in the reports is that even after the house was vacant, neighbors reported disturbances. Noises, specifically the sounds of sobbing and crying, emanated from inside, and the fire alarm repeatedly went off without explanation. Tired of the commotion and fearing that whatever energy was in there might spread to their own homes, the neighbors convinced the absentee homeowner to take action. The solution? A trio of Buddhist monks arrived at the home one night to perform an exorcism and blessing to rid the house of whatever evil resided inside.

But it didn't work. Despite laboring tirelessly throughout the night, the monks couldn't gain traction with the dark energy, and in the early hours of the morning, they finally fell into an exhausted sleep in the living room—only to wake hours later in the garage with no idea how they had relocated.

Others who are invited into the house to perform routine maintenance have had eerie experiences. One plumber was so frightened by the sight of a girl in a black dress standing behind him, when he was sure he was in the house alone, that he ran out and told the homeowner he would never step foot inside again.

The most discussed feature of the home's exterior is the number of large boulders placed in the front yard: five in the parking strip between the sidewalk and the curb and two more behind the black iron fence that encircles the front yard. (By some accounts, there was at one time an eighth boulder.) According to those who believe the tales, the boulders were blessed by the monks who attempted the exorcism and left on the property in order to contain the spirits said to haunt the house. Or perhaps they are there to prevent the spirits from returning. Apparently, there is one boulder for each of the murder victims, which begs the question: Just how many people have died in the house?

With a lack of credible information, it's difficult to answer any question about the property, let alone this one. But there are no reported deaths or acts of violence associated with the house, and none of the claims of activity can be verified. Many elements of the story seem to be easily explained away with a little critical thinking: if the home is occupied, it's not unusual that a resident might wish to be left alone, especially in a house with such a reputation, or at least use security cameras and floodlights to discourage people from trespassing. If no one is, in fact, living there, there's a significant reason why a house may be left vacant, even for decades, and it has less to do with ghosts and more to do with the benefits of owning an investment property in San Jose's high-priced real estate market. Even the boulders out front have a practical application as barriers between the front yard and errant vehicles on such a busy, accident-prone intersection.

So the questions remain: How did the legend start? And why has it persisted? Despite the lack of evidence to the contrary, might there be a grain of truth to the stories of murder and bloodshed? Might the house be harboring negative energy that is perceived by sensitive individuals and continues to fuel the rumors and wild speculation? Unfortunately, there are no ready answers. The Hellyer House may not be the "Senter of Hell"—it may not be haunted at all—but it certainly deserves its reputation as one of the city's most notorious homes.

DOERR-STEINDORF NEIGHBORHOOD

The house is small and unexceptional, tucked away among others just like it: compact, single-story homes with single-car garages. A busy intersection is nearby, and throughout the day, the sounds of traffic permeate what otherwise might be a quiet street. In one house in this neighborhood, the quiet is also disrupted by a lonely ghost.

For twenty years, Maxine lived alone in this house. Her grown children lived on their own but were troubled, involved with selling and using drugs, and they frequently came back to cause problems for their mother. Maxine tucked herself away in the little house among the trinkets she liked to collect, living almost as a hoarder would, perhaps believing that her belongings would provide her with companionship and protection from her sons. She was "unhappy," current resident Windy told me, "sweet and neighborly but lonely." Eventually abandoned by her deadbeat sons, Maxine was sometimes checked on by her neighbors. When no one had seen her for a few days, they called for a well check. Police discovered she had passed away in her bedroom some time before. The house was cleaned, sold and rented to Windy and her husband, Doug, around 2006. They didn't expect that, after having their son a few years later, there would actually be four people in the home: three living, one dead.

Windy and Doug first realized that something was amiss when they heard their toddler son chatting away in his room at night and after naps. Children frequently talk to themselves, but their son told them that he was talking "to Max." After hearing the history of their house from neighbors, Windy knew that the previous owner had never left the home and was appearing to her young son.

Maxine isn't shy about making her presence known to the family, and despite some passive-aggressive behavior, it almost seems like she's grateful that they acknowledge and accept her. Windy reports that Maxine's most frequent antics include moving or hiding items, such as small kitchen tools or pieces of jewelry that Windy, an artist, is working on. But she's cooperative when Windy asks her to return whatever is missing. Things turn up in other rooms, in drawers, on shelves—"places where they should never be," Windy says. But "she makes it so we can find them."

Maxine also registers her displeasure with the family or tries to get their attention in more dramatic ways. She knocks things off the wall or pushes items over, such as the broom in the kitchen. Everyone in the family has experienced moments when all is quiet and then a crashing noise or something falling reminds them they're not alone.

If the kitchen is where most of the activity occurs, Maxine seems to respect the boundary of Windy and Doug's bedroom. She will knock things over but doesn't take any items from there. However, one aspect of the family's life in which boundaries don't seem to matter is with Windy and Doug's son, who has been speaking to her since toddlerhood and still sees her to this day. "When he was little he used to love Maxine," Windy says, but now that he's older, her visits have become, understandably, a little disturbing. Maxine comes to see him on "a fairly regular basis," sometimes appearing in his dreams, and when he wakes, she's there. He's asked her to leave him alone, but clearly Maxine's interest in him outweighs her respect for his request, because she has returned again and again.

The family isn't frightened of sharing their home with Maxine's ghost. Windy and Doug are both unusually receptive to spirits and seem to have passed that trait down to their son. It is time for them to move on from the house, though, and Maxine seems to know that they won't be living there much longer. It seems to make Maxine sad, Windy thinks, as she has been quieter than normal lately. For Maxine's sake, we can only hope that the next family who moves in is as welcoming and understanding as the family with whom Maxine has spent the past fifteen years. Even if they're not, "she's just part of the house," Windy says. "She'll be fine."

It won't surprise anyone who has heard bumps in the night that residential hauntings are the most common type of haunt. They often occur when, as in the case of Maxine, a former resident remains attached to the house they once called home. Sometimes, a family member might experience the apparition of a loved one. At other times, those currently living in the home remain blissfully unaware that they are sharing their space with the dead. Just as one can't judge a book by its cover, haunted houses can't always be identified by looking at the outside. This means that the unassuming house next door to you might be more haunted than you'll ever know.

BIBLIOGRAPHY

General Works

Dwyer, Jeff. *Ghost Hunter's Guide to the San Francisco Bay Area*. New Orleans, LA: Pelican Publishing, 2011.

Hauck, Dennis W. *Haunted Places: The National Directory: Ghostly Abodes, Sacred Sites, UFO Landings, and Other Supernatural Locations*. 2nd ed. New York: Penguin, 2002.

May, Antoinette. *Haunted Houses of California: A Ghostly Guide to Haunted Houses and Wandering Spirits*. 2nd ed. San Carlos, CA: Wide World Pub Tetra, 2004.

Smith, Barbara. *Ghost Stories of California*. Vancouver, BC: Lone Pine Publishing, 2000.

Preface and Introduction

Bacich, Damian. "Native Americans of the San Francisco Bay Area: The Ohlone, Part 2." The California Frontier Project. Last modified April 30, 2018. https://www.californiafrontier.net.

Online Etymology Dictionary. "Ghost." Last modified 2021. https://www.etymonline.com.

1. Local Landmarks

HAYES MANSION

Diaz, Daniel. Email interview with author. May 2, 2021.

Guinn, J.M. "Mrs. Mary Hayes-Chynoweth." Santa Clara Biographies. Last modified 2014. https://freepages.rootsweb.com/~npmelton/genealogy/scbchy.htm.

Hayes Mansion. "The History of Hayes Mansion." Last modified October 15, 2020. https://hayesmansion.com.

National Register of Historic Places. Inventory—Nomination Form. National Archives. June 25, 1975. https://catalog.archives.gov/id/123861695.

Newlin, Nancy L. *The Gem of Edenvale*. San Jose, CA: Renasci Publishing, 2005.

U.S. National Park Service. "Hayes Mansion." Last modified January 24, 2018. https://www.nps.gov/places/hayes-mansion.htm.

Wisconsin Historical Society. "Mary Hayes-Chynoweth, Psychic Healer." Last modified July 6, 2012. https://www.wisconsinhistory.org.

WINCHESTER MYSTERY HOUSE®

Dickey, Colin. *Ghostland*. New York: Viking, 2016.

Dowd, Katie. "Everything You Think You Know About the Winchester Mystery House Probably Isn't True." SFGate, October 30, 2021. Last modified May 17, 2018. https://www.sfgate.com.

Ignoffo, Mary J. *Captive of the Labyrinth: Sarah L. Winchester, Heiress to the Rifle Fortune*. Columbia: University of Missouri, 2012.

Norman, Michael, and Beth Scott. *Historic Haunted America*. New York: Tor Books, 1996.

Ott, Tim. "Sarah Winchester." Biography. Last modified February 1, 2018. https://www.biography.com.

Winchester Mystery House. "History." Last modified October 9, 2019. https://www.winchestermysteryhouse.com.

CHUCK E. CHEESE

Huguenor, Mike. "Ghost Stories: TV Ghost Hunter and SJ Native Weighs Silicon Valley's Most Famous Haunts." San Jose Inside. Last modified October 31, 2020. https://www.sanjoseinside.com.

Pizarro, Sal. "If Chuck E. Cheese Goes Away, so Does a Bit of San Jose History." *San Jose (CA) Mercury News*, June 27, 2020. https://www.mercurynews.com.

Reynolds, Dave. "'To Seek Out New Life' and Millions of Dollars." *Spartan Daily* (San Jose, CA), April 13, 1978.

KELLEY PARK / HAPPY HOLLOW

Backpackerverse. "10 Scariest Haunted Things to Do In San Jose This Weekend." Last modified October 3, 2019. https://backpackerverse.com.

Dobkin, Marjorie. *Preliminary Historic Architectural Evaluation* (Draft). San Francisco, 1995. https://historysanjose.org/wp/wp-content/uploads/2011/05/KelleyHouse_DobkinHill.pdf.

Happy Hollow Park & Zoo. "Our History." Last modified 2019. https://happyhollow.org.

History San José. "History." Last modified 2020. https://www.historysanjose.org.

Marian, Sara. "Kelley Park." Clio: Your Guide to History. January 7, 2017. https://www.theclio.com.

YouTube. "Historical Kelley House—Fly Through." September 22, 2016. https://www.youtube.com.

2. Schools

ARBUCKLE ELEMENTARY

History San José. "History." Last modified 2020. https://www.historysanjose.org.

Merge Conceptual Design. "Story Road Northbound—Stories & Fairytales." Last modified September 26, 2014. https://mergeconceptualdesign.com.

SFGate. "Police Arrest Suspect in Boy's Stabbing Death." September 18, 1996. Last modified February 2, 2012. https://www.sfgate.com.

BIBLIOGRAPHY

BERNAL INTERMEDIATE

Boulland, Michael. *Whoppers and Ghostly Tales from Rancho Santa Teresa*. San Jose, CA: Santa Teresa Press, 1996. http://www.harker.com/History/PDF/Booklets/WhoppersandGhostlyTalesfromRanchoSantaTeresa.pdf.

Furlow, Jack C. "ECV1850 Plaque: The Bernal Adobe Site and Bear Tree Lot." Mountain Charlie Chapter No. 1850. Accessed March 15, 2021. https://www.mountaincharlie1850.org.

DEL MAR HIGH

The Union. "Five Haunted Places Near You." Last modified November 3, 2015. https://mhstheunion.com.

INDEPENDENCE HIGH

Bengford, Jeff. Personal interview with author. San Jose, California. May 30, 2021.

Dodd, Kellye. Personal interview with author. San Jose, California. May 30, 2021.

NOTRE DAME HIGH

Bil Ratzlaff, Karen. "The O'Connors...a Lifetime of Philanthropy." Sisters of Notre Dame De Namur. Last modified February 17, 2013. https://snddenwest.org.

King Library Digital Collections. "1890 Myles P. O'Connor Residence." San Jose, California. Accessed April 3, 2021. https://digitalcollections.sjlibrary.org.

———. "O'Connor Sanitarium." San Jose, California. Accessed April 3, 2021. https://digitalcollections.sjlibrary.org.

Notre Dame High School. "Heritage & Traditions." Last modified 2016. https://www.ndsj.org.

San Jose (CA) Mercury News. "Orphans Grieve As for a Mother," March 3, 1915.

Silver Creek High

YouTube. "Ghost Boy Scream Caught on Camera!!" December 22, 2016. https://www.youtube.com.

Slonaker Elementary

Bay Area Census. "Santa Clara County—1970–1990 Census Data." Accessed April 28, 2021. https://www.bayareacensus.ca.gov.

Online Archive of California. "Guide to the Harry E. Slonaker Papers 1989.140." Last modified September 15, 2011. https://oac.cdlib.org.

3. San Jose State University

Analla, Tiffani. "Arsonist Suspected in Joe West Fire." *Spartan Daily* (San Jose, CA), May 2, 2001.

Bay City News. "Cause of Death Not Determined for SJSU Student." SFGate, November 10, 2003. Last modified January 13, 2012. https://www.sfgate.com.

Carder, Justin. "Student Falls to Death from Joe West Dorm." *Spartan Daily*, September 25, 1995.

Herhold, Scott. "The Red Brick Dorms at San Jose State Come Down." *San Jose Mercury News*, December 1, 2016.

Myllenbeck, Kristi. "SJSU Ghosts Dying to Tell Their Stories." *Spartan Daily*, October 31, 2013.

Rhoden, William. "For 66 Years, a Force for Judo in the United States." *New York Times*, April 1, 2012.

San José State University. "Facts." Last modified March 30, 2021. https://www.sjsu.edu.

Tucker, Elizabeth. *Campus Legends: A Handbook*. Santa Barbara, CA: Greenwood Press, 2005.

Yamaichi, Jimi. "94-Year-Old Jimi Yamaichi Recalls San Jose's Japantown & WWII Internment." In *Journeys of Discovery with Tom Wilmer*, by Tom Wilmer. San Luis Obispo, CA: KCBX, March 7, 2017.

4. Hotels

SAINTE CLAIRE HOTEL

History of Santa Clara County. "George Scherrer." Last modified 2016. https://www.mariposaresearch.net/santaclararesearch/SCBIOS/gscherrer.html.

Metro Silicon Valley (San Jose, CA). "Spared the Axe." Last modified July 9, 1997. https://www.metroactive.com/papers/metro/07.03.97/cover/saved-9727.html.

THE FAIRMONT

Bengtson, John. "Chaplin's San Jose Day Making a Night Out." Chaplin-Keaton-Lloyd Film Locations (and More). Last modified July 13, 2017. https://silentlocations.com.

Fox, Frances L. *Luis María Peralta and His Adobe.* San Jose, CA: Smith-McKay, 1975.

Historical Marker Database. "The Burning of San Jose Chinatown." Last modified January 5, 2020. https://www.hmdb.org.

Learmonth, Michael. "Heartbreak Hotel." *Metro Silicon Valley.* Last modified March 5, 1997. https://www.metroactive.com/papers/metro/02.27.97/hotel-metro1-9709.html.

Parks, Shoshi. "The Fairmont Hotel Was Built on the Ruins of a Chinatown." SFGate, May 30, 2021. https://www.sfgate.com.

Stanford University. Market Street Chinatown Archaeological Project. Last modified April 16, 2019. https://marketstreet.stanford.edu.

LE BARON HOTEL / HOLIDAY INN SILICON VALLEY

Frater, Jamie. *Listverse.com's Epic Book of Mind-Boggling Top 10 Lists: Unbelievable Facts and Astounding Trivia on Movies, Music, Crime, Celebrities, History, and More.* Berkeley, CA: Ulysses Press, 2014.

Ghostly World. "Le Baron Hotel." Last modified December 7, 2012. https://www.ghostlyworld.org.

Sirica, Jack. "Far from Fleeing, Guests Are Flocking to Meet Spirit of 538." *San Jose Mercury News*, February 3, 1982.

5. Restaurants and Nightlife

65 POST STREET / SPLASH VIDEO DANCE BAR

Bollini, Chris. "Paranormal Investigators Make Contact with Spirits at Nightclub." ABC7 Chicago. October 30, 2020. https://abc7chicago.com.

Carlson, Eric. "El Dorado St.—1898." Soft Underbelly of San Jose. Last modified January 7, 2006. https://www.sanjose.com/underbelly.

TRIALS PUB

Facebook. "Preservation Action Council of San Jose." Accessed April 15, 2020. https://www..facebook.com.

Trials Pub. "About Trials Pub." Last modified 2013. https://www.trialspub.com/abouttrials.html.

GRANDVIEW RESTAURANT

BikeMaster. "History of Mount Hamilton Road." Accessed May 15, 2021. http://bikemaster.org/road-history/mt-hamilton/mt-hamilton-road-history.htm.

Mount Hamilton GrandView. "Our History." Last modified September 27, 2018. https://www.grandviewsanjose.com.

Smith, Kiona M. "The James Lick Telescope Is Built Over the Grave of Its Namesake." *Forbes*, January 8, 2018. https://www.forbes.com.

JOSE THEATRE / SAN JOSE IMPROV

Cinema Treasures. "Jose Theatre." Last modified 2021. https://cinematreasures.org.

Johnson-Reyes, Anjelah. *Ghost Stories with Anjelah* (podcast). "The Haunted San Jose Improv." February 9, 2021.

6. Parks

SANTA TERESA SPRINGS / DOTTIE'S POND

Evergreen Mural Walk. "The Legacy of Antonio Chaboya." Last modified May 1, 2016. https://www.evergreenmuralwalk.com.

Santa Clara County Parks. "Bernal-Gulnac-Joice Ranch." Accessed March 10, 2021. https://www.sccgov.org.

ALMADEN WINERY PARK

Almaden Vineyards. "About Us." Last modified 2021. https://www.almaden.com/about-us/.

Friends of the Winemakers. "About Us." Last modified 2021. https://www.fowca.org.

Friends of the Winemakers (blog). "Almaden Winery." November 15, 2009. https://fowca.blogspot.com.

History San José. "San Jose Historical Museum Association News." Last modified December 1982. https://historysanjose.org/wp/wp-content/uploads/2014/02/1982dec_sjhma_newsletter.pdf.

ALUM ROCK PARK

Danielson, Lindsey. "Using GIS to Analyze Relationships to Explore Paranormal Occurrences in the Continental United States." Saint Mary's University. Accessed May 26, 2021. https://www.gis.smumn.edu.

Hartesveldt, R.J., and H.T. Harvey. *Cultural and Natural History of Alum Rock Park*. San Jose, California, 1972. https://www.sanjoseca.gov/home/showdocument?id=31883.

Rosa, Craig, and Robin Marks. "Exploring Alum Rock Park." *KQED.* March 7, 2008. https://www.kqed.org.

Thompson, Judy. "Alum Rock Park History." *New Neighborhood Voice* (San Jose, CA). Last modified 2003. https://www.nnvesj.org.

7. Roads

QUIMBY ROAD

Backpackerverse. "10 Most Haunted Hiking Trails in Santa Clara County." Last modified October 3, 2019. https://backpackerverse.com.

Evergreen Mural Walk (blog). "Evergreen's Own Mayor Quimby." June 22, 2016. https://www.evergreenmuralwalk.com.

———. "Quimby Road—History." September 7, 2016. https://www.evergreenmuralwalk.com.

Jones, Senator Herbert C. The First Legislature of California. California Senate, 1950. Golden Gate University School of Law. Digital Commons. https://digitalcommons.law.ggu.edu/caldocs_senate/237.

McKay, Leonard. "The First State Legislature." San Jose Inside. February 13, 2006. https://www.sanjoseinside.com.

HICKS ROAD

Allan, Laura. "Rumors of the 'Hicks Road Colony' Have Kept Drivers Away from the Area for Years." Ranker. April 10, 2020. https://www.ranker.com.

Backpackerverse. "Your True Nightmare: Blood Albinos of Hicks Road." Last modified October 3, 2019. https://backpackerverse.com.

Reddit. "Albinos on Hicks Road." Last modified 2018. https://www.reddit.com.

Valley of Heart's Delight (podcast). "Episode 1(ish): The Blood Albinos of Hicks Road." August 30, 2019.

8. New Almaden

Baxter, Stephen. "New Almaden Cemetery Traces Ghastly History." *San Jose Mercury News*, November 3, 2009.

Boulland, Michael, and Arthur Boudreault. *New Almaden.* Charleston, SC: Arcadia Publishing, 2006.

La Forêt Restaurant. "About Us." Last modified 2018. https://www.laforetrestaurant.com.

Monaghan, Kitty. Phone interview with author. March 30, 2021.

Veale, Liza. "The Real History behind Mary Ellen Pleasant, San Francisco's 'Voodoo Queen'." *Crosscurrents*. KALW. September 9, 2015. https://www.kalw.org/show/crosscurrents.

9. Private Homes

Abreau-Campen, Windy. Phone interview with author. May 6, 2021.

Jerkovich, Marilyn. Phone interview with author. March 13, 2021.

Zillow. "553 Hellyer Ave, San Jose, CA 95111." Accessed March 10, 2021. https://www.zillow.com.

ABOUT THE AUTHOR

Elizabeth Kile has been interested in ghost stories since she was a child. A lifelong resident of San Jose, she is deeply familiar with all the places she's written about, from driving Hicks Road as a teenager to attending graduate school at San Jose State University. She has participated in paranormal investigations in Truckee, California, and Virginia City, Nevada, and has explored haunted locations and graveyards in almost all fifty states. She is currently a high school English teacher in San Jose, and she lives with her husband, two daughters, a coonhound named Miss Marple and a part-time cat.

Visit us at
www.historypress.com